Think like
The Minimalist

Think like
The Minimalist

Master the Art and Science of Crafting
Thought-Provoking Design

CHIRAG GANDER AND SAHIL VAIDYA

PENGUIN
BUSINESS

An imprint of Penguin Random House

PENGUIN BUSINESS

Penguin Business is an imprint of the Penguin Random House group of companies
whose addresses can be found at global.penguinrandomhouse.com

Published by Penguin Random House India Pvt. Ltd
4th Floor, Capital Tower 1, MG Road,
Gurugram 122 002, Haryana, India

First published by The Write Place 2022
Published in Penguin Business by Penguin Random House India 2024

ISBN 9780143473008

Typeset in Bembo Std by Manipal Technologies Limited, Manipal
Printed at Replika Press Pvt. Ltd, India

www.penguin.co.in

This book is dedicated to all Minimals who have worked closely with both of us ever since our inception to produce the content that has won millions of hearts.

Acknowledgements

There are several people who have helped us in this beautiful journey. We're deeply indebted to our parents (Mr. Shashank Vaidya, Mrs. Kavita Vaidya, Mr. B. L. Gander and Mrs. Deepa Gander) and siblings, especially Mr. Himanshu Gander who has been a big supporter of our vision. Without our family's support, our dream of building The Minimalist would have been stillborn. We are extremely grateful to all of them, especially Mr. Shashank Vaidya, who has been a mentor to us throughout this fulfilling journey.

We are grateful to Shivangi Ratra (Sahil's better half who nudged us to write this book) and Astha Agarwal (Chirag's better half) for all of their support and encouragement. We are also thankful to all our minimals who have been a part of The Minimalist's journey ever since our inception in 2015, without whom we would not have created a lot of the work we have presented in this book. We thank our clients who have given us an opportunity to work with them and help our philosophy grow and flourish.

We are appreciative of Nitin, for having tirelessly worked on the book design as well as many of the smart ideas that you'll find in it; Mr. Debashis Sarkar and Mr. Sourabh

Mishra for advising us through the journey and sharing critical feedback for this book; our batchmates, the entire IIT Bombay fraternity and the Techfest, IIT Bombay team for providing constant encouragement, guidance and support, without whom Chirag would not have been able to pursue a career in design; Anurag and Abhishek Mazumdar, for helping us to grow our brand of minimalism in the initial days of the journey; and Preeti, Manish, Anup, Ketan, Harshil, and Yusuf for patiently working with us through this process and making this book a reality.

Contents

CHAPTER 1

Genesis

At the end of 2018, the world woke up to a shocking piece of news. A whale was found dead on the coast of Indonesia with many kilograms of plastic waste in its stomach. Bags, bottles, cups, sandals—all kinds of plastic items were found, shedding light on the dangers of ecological degradation. The internet erupted with alarming conversations of all sorts and many megabytes of data went into writing about this heart-rending catastrophe. Many social media users were goaded into checking what the conversation was all about, owing to the sheer amount of information being circulated by way of lengthy news pieces, articles, blog posts and Twitter threads.

It is at this point that even we decided to chime in, albeit a little differently. You see, we are big believers in the fact that less is more; and when the situation came to our notice, we got thinking: what is the best way to bring this issue to light? The long news articles and blogs describing the event in great detail are certainly valuable, but to ensure that the conversation reaches far and wide, there is an immediate need for a piece of communication that is simple yet thought-provoking: in a way that the user feels compelled to ponder upon the issue and read more about it.

That is exactly what we wished to achieve, and after hours of ideating, brainstorming, designing, tweaking, re-tweaking and putting on the finishing touches, here's what we ended up creating:

Plastic – the perfect weapon for killing whales

'Wait, what? How's putting out a picture of just a whale on a red background thought-provoking in any way?'

That's what one person said while being the unwitting subject of a simple user-testing process when he first saw this idea.

If you didn't think that way and got the point of the communication in one glance, we congratulate you. But if you did, don't worry, because the entire point of this idea is extremely simple and shall be deconstructed in less than a minute.

Once pointed out, you'll never be able to look at this design in the same way, and you might even kick yourself for not noticing it earlier.

Look at the design once again and read what the caption says. Can you see something beyond just the whale?

Hidden subtly, just slightly beyond the view of the regular eye, is a **plastic bottle**. Can you see it now? If you can't, let us give you yet another hint: focus your attention on the mouth of the whale. It won't take much time now to realise that it represents the shape of a bottle! That was a neat trick by the cunning designer—using the mouth to hide a hidden interpretation!

With one swoop, this piece of content has managed to communicate a simple idea—plastic ingestion (more specifically, the ingestion of *plastic bottles* in this case) is killing whales. But without resorting to something very long or detailed, the designer has done what she does best—capture one's attention with the sophistication of simplicity and delight the senses with the art of minimalist design.

This design was posted on our Instagram account (@theminimalist_india) on 27 November 2018, and went on to break the internet. Tens of thousands of people engaged with this organically in just a couple of days. But more than our own page, the impact was felt across other channels as this very design started doing the rounds on platforms as diverse as LinkedIn, Reddit and Whatsapp. For a change, disgruntled millennials in family groups were seeing something interesting.

This, in a nutshell, is the 'Minimalist' approach.

In a world inundated with content, attention spans will continue to nosedive. Faced with this daunting prospect, every new voice on the internet wishing to be noticed has to bring *something* special to the table. Minimalism cuts right to the heart of the message and it doesn't demand much from the user, seeking only to inform, educate or entertain, which is exactly why it works.

Minimalism is a truly potent tool to build compelling communication as well as 'viral' content—things that end up being the very foundations of a brand. We first put this idea to use in 2014, and it led to the genesis and rapid growth of our company—The Minimalist. Incidentally, it was the first out of the many brands that we had ended up building.

Initial Days

The two of us—then engineering undergraduates at the Indian Institute of Technology, Bombay, met by chance and ended up spending the summer of 2014 sharing auto rides as we travelled together. Both of us were interning at the same location but in different companies. One of us was in an advertising agency, honing his design skills while the other one was whiling away precious moments of his life in a software company, having free coffee to stay awake, and diligently practicing the art of doing nothing. It was purely out of economic considerations that we ended up traveling together; deprived of an internship stipend, we did all we could to cling on to our meager pocket money. This simple decision would soon turn out to be serendipitous and change the trajectory of both our lives.

In the course of those bumpy rickshaw rides, we'd often chat about social issues that were plaguing the country. Being a big dog lover, Sahil once remarked that people hit street dogs for no reason. In response, Chirag suggested that they could make a design to highlight this issue and post it on social media. The suggestion seemed interesting. Chirag had been quite popular in IIT Bombay circles for his exploration of minimal designs which had been doing the rounds on Facebook—when organic reach on social media platforms wasn't yet martyred. If a similar approach could be taken on this issue, it could actually turn out to be quite unique and popular.

But from that idea, we started thinking about the larger philosophy of talking about issues using minimalism. Why was this particular philosophy so impactful in the first place? Da Vinci had famously remarked, 'Simplicity is the ultimate sophistication', and his pithy quote has turned out to be increasingly true in a world deluged with too much content and information. Bombarded with all sorts of media, we could see the first signs of content fatigue in those days. Moreover, minimalism was not popular in India at all and we saw tremendous potential in the power of this philosophy.

Inspired to use it in the Indian context, we also noticed a painful dearth of thought-provoking communication about social issues and matters that needed to be talked about. Issues such as gender discrimination, racism, child labour and scores of other problems were begging for a public conversation on digital media, yet there was no platform in the public sphere that sought to introduce these ideas in a memorable manner.

Based on these observations, we decided to start a Facebook

page with the idea of creating simplistic and witty content on things that were happening in the country using the tools of minimalism. After coming up with a dozen bad names, Sahil finally came up with 'The Minimalist' which was immediately chosen and the page was launched on 8 August 2014. Coincidentally, Chirag got a pre-placement job offer on the very same day. In an act of calculated courage, he declined it, imagining that a meaningful path could be constructed via this endeavour. Half a decade later, one can say that the decision was quite prescient. But on the day that Chirag took that fateful decision, all we had was a unique idea and a Facebook page with two likes.

Traction

Energised and excited by this new page, we never looked back. All hours beyond college lectures during the fourth year of engineering were spent in one shanty 6 ft x 8 ft room, brainstorming ideas, conjuring vivid perceptions, researching topics and generally destroying the whiteboard as we scribbled and doodled through the nights.

Our philosophy of minimalism was catching on, as more and more people got intrigued about the content we were putting up. Here's another design that we made on the issue of racism that is widely practiced against North East Indians:

The
high five
of **UNITY**

While staring at the Indian map for a few minutes, we chanced upon this discovery. The part of the map representing seven sisters seemed to be high-fiving the rest of the area. Of course, it required us to squint and alter our perception a bit to finally arrive at this design—and the result was heartwarming. Our audience was blown away by the observation and this got shared over a hundred times—a big feat for a new Facebook page on the block. People we didn't know were sharing our content on groups we weren't aware of, and appreciative messages highlighting how simple yet astute our observations were inspired us to stay the course.

The page's audience grew steadily and reached a few thousand followers, but the floodgates were opened when one of our content pieces on Diwali got widely shared by various content platforms, listicle websites and even news websites. CNBC Awaaz ended up featuring us on their website. The Logical Indian, a platform for meaningful conversations on the state of affairs in the country, featured our content on their Facebook page and within a few days, we had a following of over 10,000 people. From this point, there was no looking back. With every piece of breaking news, we kept coming up with our own minimalistic take which did the rounds on various social media platforms as The Minimalist's popularity soared.

It was around half a year since we'd started this page when we got a call from a startup founder who had recently raised a round of funding. She had come across our work and was interested in knowing if we could use the same creativity in helping her build her healthcare brand. Spotting an opportunity to apply our philosophy in a business context, we dived head first into the project. Despite not having any professional experience, we entered the arena with a fresh pair of eyes and learned a lot of things as we executed. Work brought more work, and we started delivering multiple projects, thanks in part to the massive amount of investor money sloshing around in the Indian startup ecosystem back in 2015. What had started as a creative experiment for two young engineers, who knew they weren't cut out for engineering, was entering the realms of becoming a company of two inexperienced founders, no employees, no business plan, and only one asset that they had: the unique weapon of minimalism.

Six years on, we have now built The Minimalist into one of India's leading creative solutions companies with a team of over 170 creative minds who come to work with a single-minded focus: to produce inventive ideas and have fun while creating business impact for clients. We are proud to have partnered with top global and Indian brands including MTV, Hyatt, HDFC Bank, Tata AIG, ITC, Airtel and The Hindu, working across areas that range from brand strategy and social media marketing to User Experience (UX) and video production. These years have been nothing short of a dream run, and have given us a chance to spread our art of minimalism through our work for brands as well as our social media channels, which continue to produce new ideas for a community of 200,000+ followers. We've also attempted to share our ideas through TEDx talks, corporate workshops and college sessions. The world has certainly taken a liking to this ideology, as numerous other creators and brands have emerged over the years, espousing this exact same approach and raising the overall standard of marketing and design in the country.

We chose to share the above facts not because we've done something special or achieved anything incredible, but purely because this approach has stood the test of time and proved to be highly impactful. In creating delight through the minimalistic approach, brands (including many of our clients) have experienced an increase in brand affinity, awareness, online traffic, sales and growth in their user base. Clearly, our magic sauce has delivered splendid results for us as well as our clients. Now, we want to let you in on that secret and share everything that has helped us do this: the exact techniques, the art and science of minimalism.

The Art of Minimalism

So why exactly are we doing this? Essential to understanding our answer is the fact that idea-sharing is a non-zero-sum game. Ideas and knowledge are things which, when shared between two parties, end up enriching both. This is the beauty of knowledge—everyone wins when it gets shared, resulting in a much richer world. In building The Minimalist, we have certainly had our own fair share of inspirations and mentors, people and brands who have influenced our thinking at various points in the journey, without whom this endeavour wouldn't have existed. Having championed this approach and seen its veritable impact over the years, we feel we now owe this knowledge to India's creative community.

There is another, lesser-known motivation behind us starting The Minimalist. When it came to the world of creativity, India was never really looked up to. At least that's what we used to think, back in 2014. We strongly believed that we could change that and wanted to be one of the voices on the internet that would be known for producing content that was so ingenious that it couldn't be found in any other corner of the world—at least in the style that we created. Whether we succeeded in that naive endeavour is a separate matter, but it did egg us on to break the mould and explore unforeseen methods of communicating ideas.

We strongly believe that every such experiment inspires the entire community and lifts the prevailing form of creativity to newer heights. We have certainly seen that happen over the years, but the impact is only limited to the upper echelons of India's internet-savvy society. Beyond the tiny percentage of digital natives who are used to provocative ad campaigns and sleek UI and UX on new-age platforms, India, at large, has yet to see a total revolution in the world of creativity. This is of course going to follow only after incomes rise and more and more people use the internet to buy stuff and thereby interact with brands and digital products, but it hasn't deterred us. We have seen what is possible when new ideas hit the market, and we're positive that in some decades, India can become a pioneering powerhouse when it comes to the world of creativity, design and marketing. This book is our humble attempt to share what we have learned, in the hope that it will inspire students, enthusiasts and knowledge workers to think and create in inventive ways, and hopefully turn India into one of the hottest destinations of creativity.

There is another reason we decided to do this. In our company, we have had many creative people who joined us in the early stages of our journey and honed their craft along the way. Over time, they've grown to become extremely adept at utilising the tools and techniques of minimalism which was strikingly evident through the work they did and the growth they experienced in their careers. To create opportunities for increased exposure and growth, we have sent many of these talented team members to colleges and universities to deliver talks and sessions on these ideas, and they've always received rave reviews for the way they've engaged and educated their audiences.

The workshops spearheaded by our team members increased over time, as did the number of people in our company who were trained and became well versed with the craft. Slowly, we realised that the process by which we come up with our signature minimalistic ideas is indeed a repeatable process that uses a number of clearly defined techniques and laws that we've developed over the years. So this book is our effort at codifying this IP and turning it into an accessible guide for anyone who wants to learn exactly how it's done.

Creativity is often likened to magic, and many works of creativity often convey that impression to the viewer. However, we believe there are certain techniques that, if learned, applied and practiced can yield the same magical results for anyone with a decent skill level in design or communication. It is our endeavour that after learning the art of minimalism, the reader will not just decipher the exact ideas that went into creating the magic that we often see in the world's best communication (hence, no longer regard it as purely 'magical'), but will also develop a set of powerful techniques that shall enable them to create that very same effect themselves, thereby turning what seems like magic into a repeatable process.

For the more hands-on reader, who happens to be a student or is working in the field of visual design, UX, copywriting, marketing, social media or brand management, this book shall act as a manual that can be put to use right away.

The Lay of the Land

This book attempts to demystify the exact techniques that have helped us in our journey: right from the seemingly miraculous pieces of work you see on our social media pages to the more professional business case studies that have helped our clients achieve tremendous success.

The first few chapters outline a very high-level approach to creating communication on any topic. In advertising jargon, we call the problem statement for any communication project a 'brief'. We shall begin, therefore, by taking a quick look at how one maps out the overall journey of going from the brief to the end output.

The next chapters will dive head first into the very techniques of observation, design, execution and copywriting that have been the secret recipe behind almost all the content that you see on our page. With in-depth examples and actionable insights on how the process of execution can be fine-tuned, creative professionals can get to work right away. On the way, we have also used some sample briefs and outlined some of our approaches at the end, so that you will be able to put what you've learned into practice and see the magic of this philosophy in real time. You will also get a more detailed understanding of the philosophy behind IEF (Include-Exclude-Focus) and other tips that can be used for sharper execution of ideas.

The last section contains some extra material on interactive content, client case studies and minimalism in action for brands the world over.

CHAPTER 2

Why Minimalism?

Before we dive into the techniques of minimalism, it is important to qualify why this approach is essential. Part of the answer lies in the introduction of this book, but we shall bring to light a few more issues that make minimalism more important than ever in the current era.

With the advent of smartphones, the amount of content and advertising consumed by humans has reached stratospheric levels. It is an insight we're all too familiar with, so there would be no need to throw a statistic or two around to highlight how intense the battle for attention is.

What's interesting is that despite the fact that more money can buy more digital real-estate and consequently more attention, we have seen that it's not just the brands and organisations with deep pockets that have managed to capture the attention of the masses and build loyal communities. In fact, more and more individuals, content creators and upstart brands have built their communities from scratch with little to no money. The very fact that this has been possible says something about the incentive structure of the way today's content platforms are designed: good content that stands out can help even a nobody garner millions of eyeballs in shockingly short periods of time.

While it may sound like a truism, the implication of the insight is that all content creators need to discover how they are going to stand apart. This is exactly why a unique philosophy like minimalism has helped us create our own community, which ultimately resulted in the genesis of a business over the last seven years.

We've seen numerous big brands with large marketing budgets that have failed to create any meaningful loyalty amongst consumers. The reason is simple and one that you may know already. Consumers are on social media to consume content that caters to specific desires and appeals to certain parts of their identities. People come on social media to laugh or cry, to be educated or to get advice in a sphere of life that is important for them. This priority is dictated by their identity at that point in time—consumers who identify themselves as fitness freaks and gym-bugs would flock towards creators who add value to their lives by talking about workout ideas they didn't know, fitness hacks that they've been looking for or probably even fitness memes that lighten up the day and help them carry on.

Now, for such a consumer, there is no dearth of pages that

create content on the above lines. In such a situation, it's critical that brands differentiate themselves not just with their communication strategy (of what they will talk about) but also *how* they execute it. This is where minimalism comes in as a critical differentiating factor—a philosophy that cuts straight to the point and helps brands to stand apart and deliver the value that consumers are looking for.

However, the benefits of using the tools of simplicity are not limited to this. By sticking to such an approach for a long enough period, consumers will start identifying a brand with that particular style and before long, they'd actually look forward to its unique take on what's happening in the world. Moreover, the style will be unique to the brand and will become an identifying mark itself—a job that is typically done by the logo of the brand. Essentially, the way a brand communicates becomes a part of its identity over time and achieves a much larger association with the minds of consumers. That is exactly what is meant by 'building a brand', and our experience suggests that minimalism is quite a potent (but definitely not the only) tool that accelerates this process of forming associations and building a brand identity on digital platforms.

While these may seem to be good reasons to embark upon the journey of minimalism, there is yet another subtle advantage of using the approach. This is something that we have directly observed in the course of observing people's reactions to our work specifically. To illustrate the point, let's look at what usually happens when people see a piece of thought-provoking content. Consider this design:

Within Agra lies the Taj

This was a design we created for a competition that sought logos for the city of Agra many years ago. If you look closely at the design, you can see the word 'Agra' written in Hindi. But upon closer inspection, you will see that the word 'Taj' is written in English! The identity of the city has been captured in one really simple design which uses merely the power of smart typography to deliver the message. This idea was widely appreciated by our audience, even though it'd often take more than a mere glance to decode the design and understand it. Like all good ideas, this one unfortunately occurred to us after the deadline and unfortunately, we weren't able to participate in the competition. However, while we were showing this around to people for user testing, it did leave us with a key insight about why such ideas work.

It has been a routine observation that when people see such ideas, they initially get confused about what is being said. But after spending just a few moments staring at it (and probably being aided with the accompanying copy), the central idea suddenly dawns upon them. The impact of finally being able to see what, moments ago, was unseen is profound. It is akin to Archimedes' eureka moment in its creation of amazement and delight (minus the running-around-naked bit). Okay, we probably exaggerated it a bit, but the reaction surely exudes delight.

We've also observed that upon being enthralled by such ideas, many feel a sense of excitement and love, showing such content to their friends and colleagues: to delight them, to show them one of the most unique things that they've come across, or simply to test them and see if their powers of perception are acute enough to identify the subtly hidden message. Not all designs need to be cryptic or have a hidden meaning- but every idea that manages to provoke thought in such a manner will certainly produce delight and gain immediate traction and attention. That probably explains why many ideas start doing the rounds on various platforms. People delighted by the ingenuity are quick to take screenshots and be the first ones to share these 'finds' in their personal circles, thus triggering contagion and resulting in the success of the communication! This is the entire philosophy behind The Minimalist: creating thought-provoking ideas that capture attention and delight people.

We are not the only ones who have harnessed the power of thought-provoking ideas to create content that goes viral. A cursory analysis of some of the best brand ads reveals that many of the topmost brands like McDonald's, Coke and Zomato have used similar techniques to capture attention and get ahead of their competition.

To summarise the point, we thereby suggest that in a world full of immense clutter and endless communication, brands and content creators need a clear strategy to not just stand apart but own a unique way of communicating their ideas. It is here that the approach of minimalism shines and provides a useful tool. Moreover, it also helps in creating an association that sticks in the minds of consumers and also has the ability to cause immense contagion when utilised to create thought-provoking communication.

CHAPTER 3

The 4-Step Process of Minimalist Thinking

Having explored the merits of minimalism and how it can help one's content stand out, we shall now perform a quick overview of the process that we have been following to systematically create fresh ideas.

To begin with, the process is a theoretical overview. Examples of how that process can be put to use shall follow right after, for even we are not big fans of just dabbling with words and would much rather showcase how it can translate into tangible output.

Before laying out this process, we want the practitioner to note a few disclaimers:

a) This is a broad approach on how to go about creating

minimalistic communication and not the only way one is supposed to do it. It has worked for us and you can certainly tweak it based on your unique style.

b) Many a times, we have broken our own process and gone in the exact opposite direction. This is not a sacrosanct prescription but is better seen as a guiding principle.

c) With practice, one's dependence on this process reduces as the principles get internalised. Therefore, like any other process, this one can be honed only via hundreds of hours of practising, user testing and using feedback loops to improve the method of thinking.

d) One must keep their egos aside as the process requires the practitioner to be ready to experiment with the stupidest of ideas. You never know what will ultimately stick and ideas rarely make sense in their infancy. Therefore, one must enter with an open mind and entertain even the remotest possibilities during the phase of exploration and creation.

That said, let's head straight to the process and review some applications.

The Process

The Art of Minimalism is based on just four simple steps, namely:

1. Defining the problem (The Brief)
2. Building a mind map
3. Creating visual representations of the mind map
4. Applying the tools of minimalism

That's it. Travelling through these four steps can lead one from a problem statement to a thought-provoking idea in a structured manner. The application of each step, however, requires a lot of deep thought, exploration and experimentation. Let us break down each step one by one with an example. We shall use one of our favourites—the example of the whale and plastic bottle that we saw in Chapter 1.

Having already seen the final output, the following breakdown will help one understand that the final product is not merely the result of some 'creative magic', but the fruit of a well-thought-out process that can be repeatedly used to produce such ideas.

Step 1: The Brief

When the news articles started pouring in, the brief to our team was loud and clear:

Brief 1: A minimalistic piece of communication has to be created to highlight the fact that a whale died due to plastic consumption.

Now, the brief could have taken a different turn as well.

In our case, as you already know from what the final output is, the team decided to focus on the exact occurrence: whales being killed by plastic (bottles). The brief could, however, have been slightly different.

For instance, since the news rekindled the public's angst against excessive plastic usage and the havoc that it wreaks on the environment, we could very well have used a different brief:

Brief 2: A whale has died due to plastic consumption. A minimalistic piece of communication has to be created to highlight the highly damaging impact of plastic or to highlight how plastic is destroying nature.

The above brief could have resulted in a very different kind of communication, which is why it is important to begin with the end in mind. There have been many occasions when the final output is based on a different message—so we grant that one need not always rigidly stick to the initial brief. It is completely fine to have a few different objectives in mind so a broader exploration of ideas can be undertaken. However, it is recommended that regardless of the nature or number of objectives, they should be articulated at the beginning so as to provide a clear direction to the thinking process.

For this example, we shall proceed with *Brief 1*.

Step 2: The Mind Map

In the second step of the process, we start putting our minds to work. One of the best ways to do this is to write down all kinds of words that come to mind when we look at the brief and think about the issue.

So what comes to mind when we think of whales being killed due to plastic consumption? Go ahead and write them down on a piece of paper to practise the process real-time.

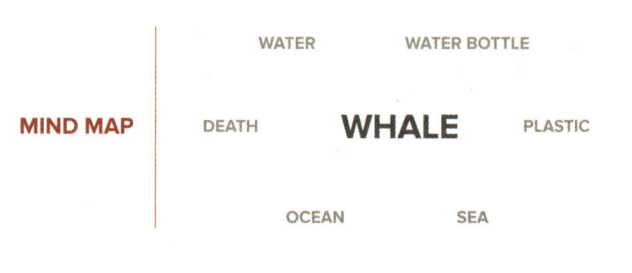

When our team was working on this, a wide variety of words were jotted down. Apart from 'whale' and 'plastic', immediate associations that came to our mind were things like water, blood, death, nature, ocean, environment, sea, shore, destruction, etc.

From here, we continued to form a list of second-order

associations: things that came to our mind when we looked at the above (first-order) list, but things that were still relevant to the original brief. These included things like the death cross, water bubbles, sand, the earth, human greed, etc.

The reason one should engage in this is to expand the mind's horizons: to put down all sorts of far-fetched possibilities in front in order to give one's self the opportunity to form associations that would otherwise have gone unnoticed or unevaluated. It is by forming these distant associations that fresh, unexplored ideas emerge, as we shall see in due time.

Step 3: Visual Representation of the Mind Map

Having written down a variety of things that came to mind, it is now time to get down to visual representations of everything on one single slate. The point is to place all objects close to each other so that the process of association can now become visual. It is here that we shall begin to mix and match things visually in order to solidify any potential connections that can lead to our final output.

The sharp reader must have noticed that we're sticking to visuals at this point, even though a lot of thought-provoking ones can easily be created without the usage of visual objects and even simply through the usage of words. Such an observation is correct, and we shall explore techniques of writing and wordplay in Chapter 7. These techniques can enable us to achieve the same objective but without having to necessarily incorporate visual design ideas, as we'll be doing in this and the next few steps.

Here are some of the visual representations of the words that came up on the mind map:

VISUALS

Some more visuals were explored and an extended mind map was created. Placing the visuals side by side, a few early glimpses of the potential end-product begin to emerge.

Step 4: Applying the Tools of Minimalism

This is where the interesting stuff begins. Having laid out the visuals in front of us, we can now begin to tinker with them and start applying some of our special tools and techniques to start moving one step closer to our objective.

For instance, one observes that there are some similarities between the shape of the whale and that of a bottle rotated to the left by 90 degrees. Can something be done by taking advantage of such a perception? Or perhaps something can be explored by drawing an association between the bottle and the sign of the tombstone?

Another thought emerged at this stage when we were actually following this process four years ago. The crack in the whale's image that represents its mouth is an interesting and oft-overlooked motif. Can it be put to clever use somehow? Is there some synergy between that part and the shape of the bottle that can be exploited? The fact that the mouth hadn't been noticed by us for so long was itself an indicator that it was a territory ripe for infusing a clever 'hidden element' in the design.

From these ideas, rough prototype sketches were created to move beyond ideation and start putting our ideas on the drawing board. A few explorations can be seen below:

TECHNIQUE

Can you show something in the negative space?

Attempts at using the technique of 'negative space' are clear in the sketch below. A plastic bottle is being hidden in the white space that is created by the tail. Further iterations of this idea lead to the insight that the perfect place to hide this bottle would actually be the mouth of the whale. Not only would it be tasteful from an execution perspective but it'd also make a lot of sense to showcase the ingestion—something that happens via the mouth of the whale.

POSSIBILITIES

This resulted in a few design variations. After a few hours of iterating, refining (which is our final step and will be explored in greater detail in Chapter 10) and user-testing, we finally came up with the whale and plastic bottle design (refer to the design on the next page).

Viewing this design now, after having traversed the four-step journey, one has a much deeper perspective. Already, the trappings of 'magical creativity' begin to fade as one sees the organised process at work. Engaging with each step deeply, one can start seeing how the logic can apply to not just this but any communication that enchants people and leads them to believe that such ideas are accessible only to a few creative geniuses and that they can only occur out of nowhere. As we have already seen, there isn't a lot of merit to such a line of thinking, for there is certainly a clear path to coming up with such ideas.

Plastic—the perfect weapon for killing whales

That said, one cannot undermine the creativity of the designer in conjuring such unusual associations and refining the execution to present the output in a classy and tasteful manner.

Having explored how the associations can be created, we shall now turn our attention to the specific tools that can be employed across briefs to create many varieties of highly creative and minimalistic content. The tool used in this example was *negative space*.

There are many more tools that we shall explore in the subsequent chapters, namely, perception shift, expressive typography, cultural referencing, humour (wordplay, sarcasm, exaggeration) and interactive content creation.

After taking a tour of all the weapons in the Minimalist Armamentarium, we shall also explore two further things that will aid you in your pursuit to create inventive content. First, we shall explore some recommendations for mastering execution and bringing in the finesse in the final stages of production which will create the 'wow' effect that everyone craves. Second, we shall offer some general suggestions on how you can improve your powers of perception and creation, so that all our ideas no longer seem like they magically descend from the clouds, but are rather the results of carefully practised and applied strategies for producing splendid results repeatedly.

CHAPTER 4

Perception Shift

Let us now begin exploring one of the first techniques of minimalism that has consistently helped us in creating those Aha! moments for people who enjoy our work: perception shift. The term is self-explanatory and has no fancy or complicated meaning attached to it.

Perception shift (PS) is simply a method of representation that creates multiple perceptions from the very same object. What it means is that the user, upon looking at the design, may actually be able to see two different things, or even more in some rare cases. At a higher level, PS can be likened to double meaning, but in design. Just like the double meaning in words uses the same expression to convey multiple meanings, a PS design attempts to showcase different visual meanings.

Combining these differing interpretations can allow us to convey hidden messages or package a message in a thought-provoking way. The eureka moment, which we described in Chapter 2, is commonly observed if the perception is slightly veiled and requires a few extra seconds for people to decipher the other perception hidden from plain sight.

If all of this seems rather abstract and difficult to grasp, we will explain it with numerous examples which will immediately allow you to see how a brief can be approached with the PS technique to produce delightful results. Let's have a look at one right away.

The most hard-hitting anti-smoking ad?

Back in 2016, while thinking about content for our Facebook page, we decided to confront one of the biggest social issues that continue to ail society—smoking. Not only is it a gigantic issue, but it also seems like most of the marketing dollars spent on communicating its ill effects seem to be going nowhere.

We keep seeing advertisements, hoardings, posters, etc., exhorting how one should quit. Cigarette packs themselves have extremely unappealing pictures of the consequences of smoking too much. However, all of this hasn't done much to deter people or even get them to think about the issue and consider a change in behaviour. The reasons seem to be multifold.

To begin with, it is a fact of human nature that when we see some warning signs appear very regularly, we start ignoring them. We believe that something similar has happened with anti-smoking communication. Second, it has to do with the quality of the messaging in anti-smoking messages.

In this regard, we believe that a lot of the communication efforts aren't compelling enough to make the target audience (i.e., smokers) even engage with the communication, leave alone think about acting on it.

Given the nasty nature of this problem, we thought we could at least try to create something in our signature style that would provoke people to take a step back and think. We understand that expecting a massive behavioural change solely on the basis of communication is a tall order. But let that not be an excuse to not come up with slightly more provocative stuff that might just end up doing a better job! With this naive thought, we tried to create an anti-smoking ad that's unlike most others doing the rounds. If you're a smoker, we promise you: it'll hit you deep down inside.

Smoking causes Erectile Dysfunction

This has been one of our most provocative pieces to date and the response has been tremendous. We even presented this design in a TEDx talk in 2017, and this was met with guffaws by a lot of the smokers in the audience. Clearly, it had done something to them. We actually had to take a five-second pause in our talk after this slide because one of the gentlemen in the audience just couldn't stop laughing!

Anecdotes aside, this design is a clear demonstration of the technique of perception shift: since you can derive two interpretations from the same visual.

Starting with the brief, we chanced upon the insight that smoking can cause erectile dysfunction. It didn't take a lot of mind mapping or visual mapping for us to realise that there was some commonality between the shape of a cigarette and that of the male genital. From there on, it was the designer's task to masterfully execute the idea—bend the shape of a cigarette so it resembles a penis while retaining its original interpretation.

To go along with this, we simply added the copy 'Smoking causes erectile dysfunction'. Many an ad copy typically attempt flourishing language. In this case, however, we decided to keep it painfully simple because the design is doing the talking and the copy had to merely support it. We shall explore more of these nuances of execution in Chapter 10.

What you just saw was one out of the three types of perception shift techniques. We shall now explore the three different types of PS approaches that can be deployed while using this approach. They are:

a) Single object, multiple interpretations

b) Internal perception shift (one interpretation inside the other)

c) External perception shift (adding an external element to produce a new interpretation)

Let us explore each of the three categories individually. To begin with, let us start with the usage of a single object to elicit multiple interpretations since we already shared an example of this technique with the anti-smoking idea.

Single object, multiple interpretations

Having already seen one example of this, let's explore a few more from our archives so we get a better sense of how it is done.

#1: Cafe Coffee Day

In July 2019, Indians woke up to the shocking news that the founder of their beloved coffee chain, Cafe Coffee Day, had ended his life. The news sent shock waves through the entire country and resulted in an outpouring of condolences from politicians, brands and the business community. At that point, we also wanted to pay our respects and came up with something out of the ordinary, instead of going the conventional way.

While thinking of ideas for the same, one of our team members was following the usual process and staring at various visuals that were associated with the man and his company. He had been staring at the logo of Cafe Coffee Day when his eureka moment happened. He had seen something that the ordinary eye would easily miss.

Here's the logo of Cafe Coffee Day:

Having seen this so many times, it is difficult for one to deconstruct the identity and look at the parts that make up the whole, for there may be interesting ideas hidden in such a view that can be harnessed by a minimalist designer. This is also one of the ways of conjuring up ideas that we shall discuss later.

For now, suffice it to say that the curious designer did exactly that and ended up looking beyond the brand name. Analysing the logo mark, it became clear that it resembled a human face (having a dialogue because that's what the identity is about apparently). The face looks rather happy and this is where the key idea struck the designer.

What if the same face, the face of the brand that was built by Mr Siddhartha over the years, could be slightly modified to suit the occasion?

What if we could tweak a few curves and modify it ever so slightly to turn the same logo into a sad face to denote the sadness that marked this dark day?

With a few careful tweaks, this was the final output:

The journey of Café Coffee Day founder V G Siddhartha has come to a sad point

This design immediately struck a chord and was shared by many who were fond of the brand. While communicating on such dark days can be a contentious issue, we decided to put this up as a way to commemorate the man and acknowledge that he had built a brand that was close to thousands of young Indians.

Now, from a technical point of view, this again falls in the same category as our anti-smoking ad: single object, multiple interpretations. With the same object, the viewer can identify not only the CCD logo but can also immediately see a sad face. To ensure that the context was not missed (considering people's familiarity with the logo that contains the brand name), our wall copy was direct and explanatory.

The reason why this particular method of PS is one of the most delightful ones is that it takes the highest amount of effort and keen observation to arrive at designs where a single visual exudes two very different interpretations. One must appreciate that it is parsimonious and sticks to the very essence of minimalism: using as little as possible, to paint multiple stories. This is why any time we come out with a clever PS design of this manner, it receives a very heartwarming response.

Here is another example of this style.

When the Indian U19 cricket team managed to clinch the World Cup, here's how The Minimalist decided to talk about the win:

One must note that the overall process to arrive at this point is exactly the same as the one described in all previous examples. To refresh your memory, it is:

Brief (Creating communication on the Indian U19 World Cup Victory)

↓

Mind map for this brief (includes words like Cricket, WC, Cup, Trophy, 19, Young, Champion, Number 1, etc.)

↓

Visual representation of all these

↓

One of the techniques of minimalism (Perception shift, in this case, identifying that '19' can be fit into the visual of the cup considering the similarity in shapes and orientations).

A clever modification of the cricket trophy allows us to see both the trophy as well as '19' represented by it.

Now let's move on to the second approach.

Internal perception shift: One interpretation inside the other

In this approach, instead of showing two interpretations with the same visual, we shall utilise an internal element of a visual object to allow a second interpretation to emerge.

Essentially, we are trying to create a sub-object that can allude to an added meaning/interpretation and thereby result in a perception shift rather than relying on one object in its entirety exuding two different interpretations. Let us once again understand this better with an example.

Being the cricket lovers that we are, we were all thoroughly enjoying the IPL T20 matches back in 2018. While doing so, we were obviously sipping chai, which happens to be India's favourite beverage. But we are not alone in the pursuit of this dual obsession. One look at all the electronic stores when India is chasing a target in a nail-biting contest and you'll see hordes of people crowding around with their cups of chai. It's the same situation in millions of homes, as people enjoy their *cutting* while relishing the joys of an exciting game.

We decided to make something based on this observation. Once again, while tinkering around with various associated visuals, we stared hard at the visual of a teacup.

All that staring resulted in yet another curious observation, as always. Look closely and you will be able to see that the grooves in the cup look eerily similar to cricket stumps! Isn't it?

The resemblance is uncanny, and from here, it was simply a matter of opening a blank canvas and creating this design to celebrate India's two obsessions:

Cricket and Chai – India's obsessions #IPL2018

Let's take a look at another example of how perceptions within an object can yield a very different perspective.

On Earth Day in 2019, we decided to put our creative lenses to work in order to come up with an idea that would be thoroughly different from all other environmental communication. To do that, we harnessed the power of what one can see very clearly with their eyes but ignores very easily. As you may have already guessed, that is exactly the kind of experience that can be created by an internal perception shift.

As with the previous example, this one required a fair deal of staring too, and this time, the designer was staring at an image of our planet.

Now, if you're like us, these images will never look the same again. When you stare at them with the perspective of someone obsessed with minimalist design, your mind starts perceiving images that are not really there. In this case, the designer was looking at the shapes of the continents on the globe and wondering: 'What do these look like? Can they be tweaked a bit to showcase something?'

At this point, a faint resemblance with the bodies of birds and animals began to appear. Yes, that might not be so obvious right now, and this is where practicing and using a few secret tools helps very much, but once the visual representations are placed side by side for tweaking and playing around, a striking possibility begins to emerge.

After hours of manipulation and finishing touches, here is what the final output looks like:

The Earth belongs to them too #EarthDay2019 #ProtectTheAnimals

Is it not fascinating to see how the protruding left part of Africa could be so naturally interpreted as a lion's mane, or how the entire map of South America could be construed as a big bird taking flight?

Following the process, utilising one of the most potent weapons from our minimalism arsenal and making the right execution of choices certainly bore fruit in this case. Needless to say, this is yet another example of internal PS, where you can see the internal components of the main object (the globe) being tweaked to create a second perception—that of animals.

Now, let us move on to the last approach.

External perception shift: Adding an external element to produce a new interpretation

In the previous approaches, we saw two different methods of PS: either using a single object as a whole to provide multiple interpretations or using elements from within the object (and not the entire object itself) to create another perception.

The external perception approach introduces an external object to the original one in order to add an extra meaning to the original object, thereby creating a second interpretation. Essentially, this method adds new elements to pre-existing objects from the outside to superimpose a second meaning.

This approach is best captured in the design that we made to congratulate the New Zealand cricket team for their victory in the World Test Championship. Here's what the design looks like (refer to the image on the next page):

Analysing this design now, it's easy to make sense of the seemingly imperceptible statements that preceded it.

Here, the main object is the logo of the New Zealand cricket team. To showcase the fact that they had done a terrific job (and bowled us out to win the cup), the designer has introduced the second element—the bails—externally.

As a result, the elements of the logo start looking like the stumps. Hence, with a simple intervention—cleverly adding a few bails at the right location— we have externally introduced a second perception to the design.

However, the external object need not be external in the strictest sense of the word. All that is necessary here is to ensure that an external element when placed adjacent to or superimposed onto the original object, results in a second meaning. As we have said earlier, perception shift is double meaning but for design, and in this particular approach, the idea is to see how the same effect can be produced by the (unusual) introduction of an external element.

You bowled us over with your performance. Congratulations NZ!

There is another example of how we used this approach to talk about the farmer's protest that recently rocked the nation.

This is unlike many of the designs that The Minimalist has created for various reasons. Before we get there, let us quickly analyse it. By now, the reader must have developed a decent understanding of the approach and can already break it down.

The main object here is the farmer's sickle. It was one of the most unique things in the visual mind map owing to its particular shape. The curve of the sickle and the ample negative space created by it give the designer enough room to play around and try various techniques to create something intriguing.

In this case, though the designer zoomed out even further to notice a meta-perception—that the sickle indeed resembled a part of the letter र (Devanagari script).

Realising that this is a part of the rupee symbol, the designer was onto something.

Clearly, the farm bill's ultimate impact will be on the income that farmers can receive for their efforts, which made it such a big issue in the first place. Therefore, by using an external element (the two lines drawn on the mud), an extra perception is ingeniously added to the main object (the farmer's sickle). In doing so, the design also cuts to the heart of the issue—are farmers going to derive monetary benefits from the new bill?

Does the new farm bill look fruitful to you?

When we came up with this idea, we decided not to announce an opinion of our own. One must also notice that the wall copy in this case is not making a statement but inviting opinions. This is an important point to note for brands and creators.

First, this is a very deep issue and requires in-depth research. We would not want to pretend that we know it all and have done our reading. In such cases, it's best to stay honest and not say something that is not backed with solid research and something that you have conviction about.

Second and more important, we still decided to create something on this issue. Many brands feel immense apprehension to put up anything on their communication channels when a controversial issue is brewing in the nation. However, by not annoucning a rigid opinion and creating content in a neutral tone, one can always join the conversation without running the risk of alienating particular groups of people or fearing any sort of backlash.

It is important for brands and creators to come across as humans, and it is a fundamental aspect of human nature to want to talk to your community about issues that matter to them. We have just showcased a neutral approach in such situations, where one can genuinely initiate discussions but also not make any mistake that harm the brand. After all, many a brand have been built solely because they chose to voice their opinions on a particular social issue, and that too in a bolder-than-usual manner.

Having gone through the three different approaches to perception shift, we shall now move on to the next tool in our kit: negative space.

But before we do that, here's a fun task that you can attempt based on what you've learned so far. Time to enter the practice nets!

Practice Net

Challenge #1: The government has just announced that plastic has been banned and anyone who is caught using plastic bags can be arrested. Come up with a compelling perception shift on the above topic.

Give it a shot, it will be fun! Even if you cannot come up with something smart, do not worry. In Chapter 11, we have shared some of our ideas in response to all the challenges, so you can see the techniques and approaches being put to use.

CHAPTER 5

Negative Space

The next trick up our sleeves, which also happens to be one of the most ingenious ways of creating ideas like a design-magician, is none other than 'negative space'. To understand this, let's first understand what the term itself means.

For this, we shall go back to the very first example that we started the book with—the whale and plastic bottle. Take a look at it once again (refer to the image on the next page).

What we see prominently in this design, at the meta-level, are two things: an image of a whale in white (the subject of focus) and the red background.

Since the designer wants you to look at the whale—which is the subject—the entire space covered by it, i.e., the entire white shape is what we would call the *positive space* in the design.

Therefore, the rest of the space around (and between) the subject—the entire red area of the background, including the region surrounding the shape of the whale—is the *negative space.*

Plastic – the perfect weapon for killing whales

This technique is all about cleverly utilising the negative space—the area of the design which is not the main subject of focus for the user—and manipulate it to hide another meaning that becomes evident upon closer inspection.

If I have to draw an analogy, negative space is nothing but a game of hide and seek! It is a battle of wits between the designer, who attempts to hide something in the negative space and the user, who attempts to locate that hidden meaning by carefully observing the design.

However, this game is different from the original one in a way that makes it all the more interesting. And here's the difference: if the user is able to seek successfully (which means that she's able to identify the hidden element and understand its meaning), then both parties win! The user experiences delight at having figured out an intelligent piece of art and so does the designer, for having achieved the object of his endeavour: using creative ingenuity to produce delight.

Let us come back from our pseudo-philosophy to the real world now and look at the design once again. If you understood the analogy, you will now see through the mechanics of this design: the whale is the subject and it is the bottle that the designer has hidden in the negative space. To do that, she has cleverly carved out a little space to depict the mouth of the whale—and it is exactly this negative space that becomes the hiding spot for the bottle—that will lend an added meaning to the design!

The trick here is that it is not hidden in the positive space. In simpler words, the bottle is not to be found in the white-coloured stuff that makes up the whale in this design and is the subject of your focus. Rather, by playing with the part of the red *background* close to the mouth of the whale (negative space), the designer ingeniously managed to show a bottle.

Having now deciphered what the cunning designer intended to do here, read the caption again, and all the pieces will now fall into place. If the designer had tried to hide the bottle in the positive space, it would probably have resulted in a perception shift idea—something we have already explored at length.

Let us look at another example. This is from the archives and was one of our first ideas that utilised this technique. Posted on Martyrs' Day, this was an attempt to pay our respects to all the Indian soldiers who had sacrificed their lives for the nation.

Ready for our game of hide and seek? Let us begin:

A silent guardian
A watchful protector
An Indian Soldier

Inside every soldier lies a hidden batman

See it?

We admit that this is not one of the easiest ones to understand. We have had to explain the idea to many a baffled viewer who came across this over the years. As you would know, if a designer has to explain his work, probably something's wrong with it! We were afraid that such was the case with this idea too, until we posted it on our Facebook page with a caption that tries to provide a hint. So yes, if you haven't figured it out yet, just look at the caption: 'Inside every soldier lies a hidden batman'.

Hmm. It's almost as if the designer is literally trying to point you to what's 'hidden'! It's a hidden batman, as stated, so jog your eye around the subject—the soldier's figure—and see if you identify a hidden something in the negative space?

Ah, there it is! Parked cosily in the negative space surrounded by the solider's gun and his arm is the logo that we all love—the batman symbol! And now it all makes sense—the batman quote being used, the hint dropped in the caption. What a fun game, is it not?

Even though it sounds fun once explained, we were still not sure if most people would get it. We decided to risk it nevertheless and see if it worked. Within minutes of posting it, we saw that a few people had won the game of hide and seek—and they shared the design as a badge of pride—that they had successfully identified it and egged their friends on to check this piece out as well. What followed was a landslide effect, with thousands of reactions pouring in, in no time! While that may hardly sound like a big number today, it was a big pat on the back for us at that time and it pushed us to come up with more of these ideas in the future.

Moreover, the crucial point here is that such clever designs achieve the exact purpose that we intend—generate contagion by turning it into a conversation. Many people who experience the aha moment feel compelled to share it in their groups or on their feeds—either to challenge people or to brag about their astute observational skills (usually these two purposes go very well together) or simply to be that person in the group who is known for sharing such thought-provoking content. Such is the power of minimalism and its techniques!

So far we have seen two examples of the usage of negative space. The commonality in these ideas was the fact that the hidden element in the design was within the confines of the subject itself. To understand this, just look back at the two designs again. The bottle for the first one and the Batman logo for the second; the hidden elements—the whale and the soldier respectively—were located *inside* the subject.

However, there's another way one can do so, and that is by combining multiple subjects to forcefully create a negative space which can then be manipulated to hide something. As with all technical explanations, an example will do best to illustrate what we mean.

So take a look at one of our recent creations, something that was used to mark the New Year's Eve at the end of 2021. As all of us have painfully experienced, the end of the year was marked by yet another surge in COVID cases, making it extremely unsafe and unfeasible to go out.

What that implied was that the New Year's Eve in 2021 would unfortunately have to be celebrated indoors. This, therefore, was the brief that the designers undertook and the concept that they came up with communicated a sombre message in the most fun and smart way possible. Take a look for yourself (refer to the image on next page).

This one's not a particularly tough game of hide and seek after all. One can clearly see a home hidden in the middle which indicates a 'Stay at home for the party' message.

What's different with this, as opposed to the previous examples, is that it has brought together two subjects, which were combined together to create the negative space and then embedded with the hidden meaning. This is how one can play around with multiple subjects and shapes, twisting, bending and combining them to conjure a negative space that can incorporate a hidden element.

Where's the party tonight? ~~At the dance floor.~~ *At home. Happy New Year!*

How one can arrive at such observations is a subject that we'll tackle in Chapter 9.

Let's now turn our attention to one last type of negative space approach. This one shall utilise typography and use written words as its subject in order to hide elements within the contours of the letters that make up the words. This example would also be relevant if it were placed in the next chapter on 'Expressive Typography', but we decided to present it here as it offers another compelling angle of attack for the designer who's keenly interested in exploiting the power of negative spaces.

Here's what our team produced on the issue of water conservation:

#WorldWaterDay

The creative simply has the word 'Save' written here—but save what? The answer to that lies in the negative space of the letter 'a'—one can see a water droplet hidden there, thereby conveying an obvious message in a not-so-obvious manner.

We can see that unlike all other cases, this one has relied on the usage of words to build the message. It is a clever combination of the subject—the word and its meaning itself—and the element hidden in the negative space to consolidate and communicate one unified meaning.

Many such possibilities exist in the realm of using letters and words to communicate powerful hidden messages. We shall explore the endless possibilities in the next chapter.

Practice Net

Challenge #2: Use the negative space approach to communicate a powerful message on wildlife conservation.

(Hint: If you're not able to come up with something, try using a deer or a penguin as a subject—there's ample opportunity to play with their shapes!)

CHAPTER 6

Typography

So far we've explored numerous ways in which visual representations of objects can be put to smart use for the purposes of provoking thought. Is the same possible by using only text? If you're like us, you can already hear yourself muttering 'Hell yeah!'

This chapter shall be our humble attempt to prove that one can create delightful design solely with the power of words, letters and the meaning one can embed by manipulating them. Words themselves contain stories, and it only requires a different kind of perception to bring those stories alive.

Sticking solely to text in order to tell a story is also taking the idea of minimalism to an even higher level—getting even more parsimonious with the tools at your disposal while producing the same end-effect as all our communication.

Don't believe us, yet? We bet you would, once you start seeing some examples. Here's one to tickle the funny bone.

If you fell off your chair or spat out the coffee, we apologise. This was the exact reaction we received when we presented

HAPPY FATHER'S DAY

this idea to our audience during a TEDx talk in 2017. Guffaws ensued right after we displayed this slide, and the effect produced by typography was evidenced by the decibel levels of the auditorium.

It's a matter of fascination to see that a mere arrangement of letters (with the ever-so-subtle tweak) can produce such a massive effect. All the designer had to do here was to tweak the apostrophe mark (something that nobody even notices while writing words, which makes this design even more creative) to make it look like a sperm cell and voila, our hilarious concept was ready.

The sharp reader must have noticed that while it does

seem like a good example of typography on the surface, the real trick here was to identify that the apostrophe sign does bear a resemblance to the sperm cell and can therefore be tweaked to create a double interpretation. And as anyone who has reached thus far in the book would be able to identify, this is straight out of our second technique: perception shift.

The observation is bang on. This design certainly uses perception shift and that is the beauty of typography: it can borrow from many other techniques to weave its magic. For that matter, even the negative space technique can be utilised with words, as we saw in the 'Save Water' design in Chapter 5.

There are various such approaches that can be used within the world of typography. There are three in particular that shall be explored in this chapter.

- Expressive Typography
- Combining with other techniques (Perception Shift and Negative Space)
- Ambigrams and Dynagrams (An IP created by The Minimalist)

All three approaches have the same overarching philosophy but take unique directions. We predominantly want to focus on the first approach as that is most easily and powerfully utilised in our experience. However, it would only be apt to also explore the other two approaches as they offer a very unique method to designers looking to break the mould within the world of typography itself. One such idea—The Dynagram—originated via such attempts to do something truly different and augment the magic of typography with the use of animation.

Let us begin our exploration and behold the possibilities presented by pure, simple textual play.

Expressive Typography

Expressive Typography (ET) is an approach that tells a story simply by arranging text in a certain order. Now you may wonder how that is possible. Just imagine: there are 26 letters in the alphabet, and each letter is made of multiple shapes. What's more, each of them can be even tweaked in various ways to attain many more possibilities. It is through this approach that we can depict objects and associations—by simply manipulating the shape, placement, curvature and orientation of the letters of the words we will utilise.

The trick behind ET is also, just like our previous techniques, to point to an additional interpretation beyond what the text represents. What this means is that it is our job as designers to create room for a second meaning to emerge from the text that we are using. Here's the first out of the many interesting instantiations of this approach.

On Doctor's Day, our team wanted to steer clear of the regular sentimental communication that has become a bit too drab (and easily gets ignored) and explore something quirky. One of the observations during the brainstorming session was that doctors are notorious for their difficult-to-decipher handwriting. This could be a potent space for exploration. The insight is directly related to text: so we thought of bringing it alive and *expressing* it textually.

Happy Doctor's Day!

See what the designer did there? The idea was expressed by the text itself—the words 'Happy Doctor's Day' were written and the word 'Doctor's' was simply mangled for hilarious effect to drive home the point: that we just can't understand what they write (Sorry doctors! We still love you). It's so simple: take the idea and let a textual manipulation express it!

While the idea does strike everyone's fancy, we acknowledge that coming up with it or even grasping how one has to go about ideating to arrive at such solutions is no mean feat. To make you grasp the approach in a slightly deeper manner, we will share a few more examples in detail, describing exactly how the idea originated in our minds before it got executed in its final form.

When Elon Musk announced his Mars mission, there was a tremendous amount of buzz online. Wanting to capitalise on the same, we got to work and wondered how we could stay true to our principles in developing our communication. We went to the drawing board, made mind maps, and sketched out several items.

The initial response that everyone had was that we could play around with a visual of Mars itself. Googling to see what the image looks like, we realised that there's nothing unique about the image; it is just a spherical visual, much like any other planet, and does not offer many opportunities for manipulation.

But everyone was also quick to observe that the planet's visual does represent the letter 'O'. This insight could be deployed by way of expressive typography. The most obvious representation of this idea would be to start searching for words in your mind map that contained O in order to create such an opportunity. The name 'Elon' itself has an O, so one might begin the exploration by replacing the O in Elon with the shape of Mars:

However, this representation didn't really appeal to us. To begin with, the attempt is not as clever as we would like it to be. Second, to make the O look like Mars would require quite a lot of effort because it could very well be perceived as the Earth (or probably not even be perceived as a planet for all you know!). Given that a mere circle without much manipulation would not really represent Mars and end up creating a sense of delight, this idea didn't seem very promising.

Additionally, this was one of the first ideas that all of us arrived at. To be sure, it is a safe assumption that the very first ideas that strike the mind are generally not the best. It is a principle that has helped us over the years and the perseverence that follows has many a time allowed much more sophisticated and smarter ideas to emerge.

Undettered, we gave this brief some more thought. 'Is there a better way to take advantage of this perception?' we thought. After some tinkering around, there was a flash of insight. Chirag, who had been trying to use his ET chops on this brief, said, 'What if we remove the O from the name and move it to the top of the frame?'.

We were all puzzled and intrigued by thought, and he already had an explanation ready. Instead of focusing on the micro-details of the news announcement (and the brief, therefore), he said that the larger picture here was about one man setting his sights on a planet in our solar system in a bid to conquer it.

Essentially, the way he looked at it, this brief wasn't about a spaceship or the peculiarities of Mars. It was about Elon Musk attempting to do what nobody was daring to do: getting to another planet. Looking at it that way, could we now tell this story by lifting the 'O' in Elon and placing it at the top-right of the screen to depict Mars?

Suddenly, it dawned upon us. Not only would this lead to a very different sort of typographical representation, it'd also hint at the unique nature of attempting to reach a planet that was far away from Earth. The designing process was fairly straightforward once we were convinced about the insight, and this is what the result looked like:

Depicted this way, it shows how this person is dedicated towards conquering the distant planet—how this man's identity has come to be defined by the thought of terraforming Mars! Needless to say, the idea immediately caught fire on social media, given the thoughtful design as well as the quick response to the trending news.

We were even more delighted when Jeff Weiner, the erstwhile CEO of LinkedIn, commented on our design:

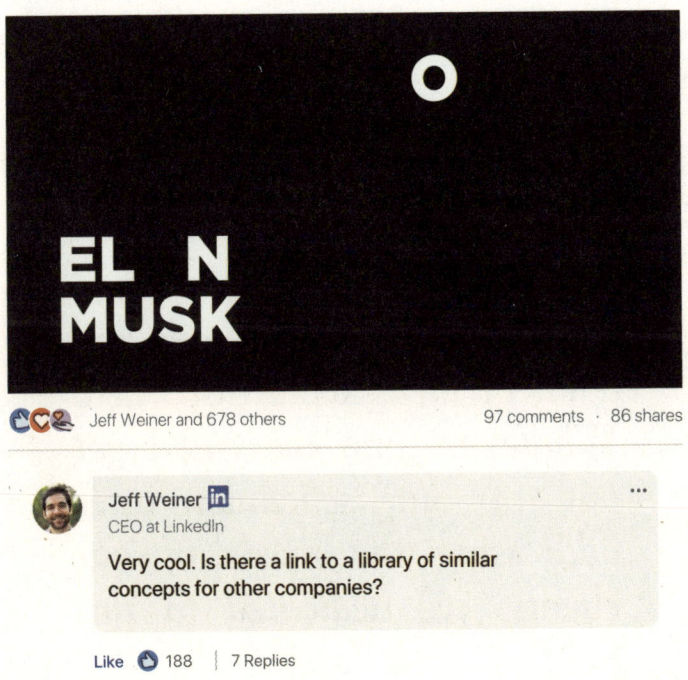

We were overjoyed to see the CEO of one of the world's biggest social media firms appreciate our work. But it wasn't enough for us. Instead of just rejoicing and moving on, we read and re-read his response. Since he had asked for similar concepts, we decided to get to work right away.

'But which company's CEO should we start with?' we thought. The easiest thing to do at this point was simply to pick the man who had appreciated our work and make something for him! Therefore, the next brief for us was to create a typographical delight for none other than Jeff Weiner.

To stay true to the theme, we wondered how we could simply use the letters we saw in his name to deliver something simple and memorable.

Many scribbles were made and a lot of ideas were discarded. Whatever time we could get out of our schedules after addressing the needs of our clients, we dedicated to this brief.

One of us went back to re-read the statement Jeff had made—to get one more look at the brief, as they say—

and that's when the insight hit us. Look at the picture on page 73 once again. Do you see the LinkedIn logo next to the man's name? Right next to it, two things immediately drew our attention. One was the 'In' written in the word 'LinkedIn' itself, but there was another 'in', that was in the man's name: the 'in' in Weiner. And therein lay our insight! Encapsulating the logo of LinkedIn in the name of the person would lead to the very idea we were looking for! This is what it came out to be (here we have presented a cleaner version of the original design):

Simple and subtle—that is how we like it.

The idea was immediately posted on LinkedIn and we hoped that he would notice this one too. Our hopes were answered with yet another note of appreciation—and it made our day! Here's what he had to say:

Jeff Weiner and 5269 others   179 comments · 72 shares

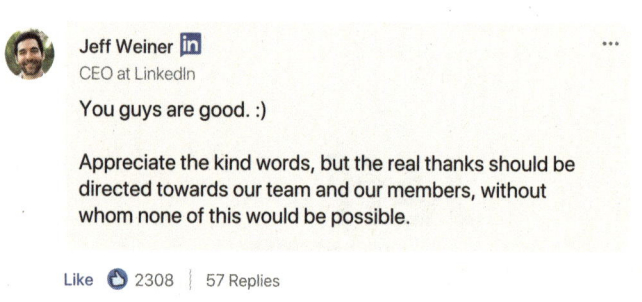

Jeff Weiner in
CEO at LinkedIn

You guys are good. :)

Appreciate the kind words, but the real thanks should be directed towards our team and our members, without whom none of this would be possible.

Like 2308 | 57 Replies

The design quickly surpassed a million views and we garnered a new cohort of followers in the US, thanks to the massive publicity created by Jeff's comment. We were humbled and delighted to see that such simple ideas were gaining so much love from different parts of the world.

We often tell students and creative enthusiasts in our talks that this example represents the power of minimalism. The ideology has the strength to captivate the topmost minds of the world and delight all kinds of people, regardless of their culture and preferences. The art of minimalism is truly global in nature, and this is just one out of the many examples which validate this statement.

While we are at it, we would like to showcase one more example of a prominent business personality who made the news and how we ended up using that opportunity to delight our community with an ET-based design. The man in question up next is one of the richest personalities on planet Earth—Jeff Bezos.

The news this time around was that he had just become the richest person in the world—at least for a while. Capitalising on the short duration for which the richest men usually retain their #1 status, we quickly came up with this (please refer to the design on the next page).

Yet again, the designer observed that the huge number of zeros that make up the hundred billion dollar figure could simply be placed next to an 'O', which she conveniently found in the word 'Bezos'. The rest, as they say, was history.

JEFF BEZ00,000,000,000$

We liked the last three designs so much that we framed them and put them up in the conference room of our office. Yes, there was a time when we went to the office and had our brainstorming sessions in a non-remote manner.

The idea was perfect, as these frames would always catch the attention of our potential clients and never fail to impress. It would elicit a lot of smiles and laughter and act as the perfect ice-breaker, leading up to a great meeting (and many deal closures too). It wasn't until we tried this that we realised how effectively minimalist design could be used as an ice-breaking tool. Go ahead and give it a shot—place this book at your desk (or coffee table) and see the warm responses and appreciation from visitors, friends and guests shoot up immediately!

We have a much more thoughtful example of ET that we had to include in this chapter. This was an idea that we came up with on the day the world lost a genius scientist by the name of Stephen Hawking.

In an attempt to pay our respects to the man, we came up with a lot of ideas and nothing really struck us as unique. The problem was compounded by the fact that most visuals that people would associate the man with were highly technical and not very popular. For instance, he was widely known for his work (Hawking Radiation, his work on black holes, etc.) and his books (*A Brief History of Time* and other titles). However, not only were these topics a tad complicated and bereft of popular appeal, they were not even conducive to any easy visual representation, thereby compounding the difficulty of coming up with anything smart to depict the man by talking about his work.

Our thoughts moved to some of the other aspects that were very well known about him: and that's when we noticed that he was differently abled, which made his stance rather unique. Unfortunately, his neck was always tilted and he had to be tethered to his wheelchair. These were two things that stood out when we looked at all his images. The one that is the most visible out of the two is, of course, the way his neck is tilted. Images typically capture only the upper half of the body so the wheelchair does get obscured, but that unique frame of his is always noticed.

In a bid to utilise this, we racked our brains hard to see if there was some way to incorproate this motif. Sahil even craned his neck multiple times to just experience that position and that is when the idea came.

It is not until you tilt your neck for an extended duration that you realise that it is not the most convenient way of being at all. But the man had to live that way for almost his entire life. Could we use this insight in a clever manner to make people not just see this fact in a design but experience it?

It was damn simple. At first it seemed a bit far-fetched but as we tested the idea, it started to make complete sense. We simply decided to write the man's name on our design but in a tilted manner. So everyone who saw the design would have to tilt their necks in order to read it clearly. It is a natural reaction. Even if we can read what's in front of us, we much prefer tilting for better clarity, and that is how we could make them empathise with Stephen Hawking. In this case, the wall copy had a big responsibility to communicate the message, and that's why it read:

'Let's feel for a second what he felt for a lifetime'

In our view, this idea was quite unique compared to the other ET examples (not to say that we differentiate between our designs—we love them all equally!). We say this for two reasons:

- It was not just a design, it created an experience for the user. Very rarely does that happen simply by using a static visual but somehow this design managed to create the desired effect

- It utilised a well-written copy which added to and complemented the core idea to create a very thought-provoking result. It can even be said that the design would be incomplete without the support of the copy, which is why it was a beautiful combination.

Here's the design:

Let us feel for a second what he felt for a lifetime. RIP, you genius

Having seen a variety of ET examples, we want to end this section with one last demonstration. We have used this idea because it is, again, slightly different from all the above ideas in one respect. The details shall be mentioned after you have had a look at it (and probably even had a nice little laugh remembering those lovely, old days)

On Teachers' Day, our team decided to use the ET approach and ended up creating something that not only invoked laughter but also brought smiles on our faces as we revelled in the nostalgia of our golden years at school.

This idea was borne out of the astute observation by one of our writers that people often make a mistake in the spelling of the phrase. They write 'Teacher's Day' whereas the correct spelling is 'Teachers' Day'. It's all about the apostrophe. A quick connection was drawn between this and how mistakes are something that teachers never miss. This further led to haunted memories of those red circles which would fill up our notebooks.

'But hey, that's exactly where the idea is,' the writer exclaimed, still recovering from the trauma of her Math homework memories. By writing a wrong spelling and circling the error with a red pen, we could create the perfect Teachers' Day post. And that's how connecting one dot to another led to this remarkable concept.

Now, we mentioned a while back that this idea was slightly different from the others. The reason behind it is simple. If you observe closely, you will realise that this is the only idea out of the pack that uses an extra element beyond just the words to produce its effect. All the other examples we saw— Elon Musk, Jeff Weiner, Jeff Bezos and Stephen Hawking— used nothing but the letters, albeit in modified arrangements,

TEACHER'S DAY

towards their end goal. This design incorporated an additional external element—the red mark.

We bring this minor point up to talk about how, in ET, it is fine to bring up such subtle elements to enhance the quality of the idea. There is no hard and fast rule governing this approach. As long as one plays around with the orientation, placement and arrangement of letters and words, it works.

We want to end the exploration of ET with one last idea. This one's special because it is not just a design that we came up with for some social issue or trending news piece. It's a logo for a company that has been in existence for more than half a decade now and is employing over a hundred people. This was one of our first branding briefs where we had complete freedom to do what we wanted to, and it is a rather fine example of the approach we have been discussing.

Here's the logo that we have been raving about:

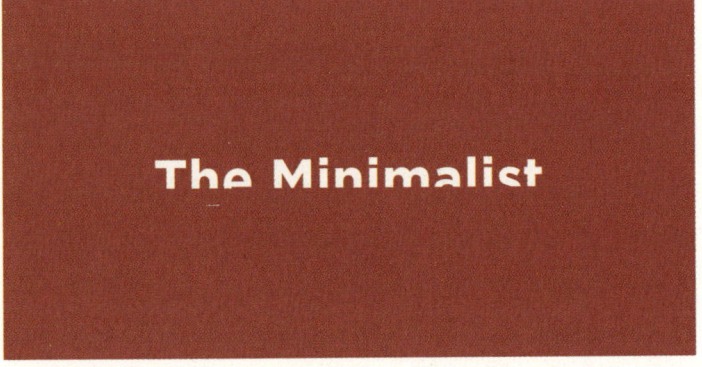

Yes, *our own logo* is nothing but a piece of expressive typography! At the time of starting our journey, we wanted to use the principles of minimalism to differentiate ourselves. Since that was a founding tenet, it was directly incorporated into the logo by being cut into half to *express* that very idea visually!

This logo holds the record for being approved in the shortest period of time in the entire history of the hundreds of brand identities we have created since then! Chirag, an amateur designer, made this in 10 minutes and sent it to Sahil who, without an iota of knowledge about how these things worked, simply said, 'Looks good, let's roll'. And that, ladies and gentlemen, is how quickly our own logo was finalised!

That makes it even more delightful because to this day, seven years later, our logo is a massive talking point for our clients, team members, partners and community members. We've had innumerable conversations where we've been asked, 'Why is your logo half cut?' The explanation never fails to bring a smile on the face of the people who ask this question, and it continues to act as a fantastic conversation starter for us. Probably that is what logos are supposed to do—not just encapsulate what the company stands for in an effective way but also pique people's interest—get them to ask what it is all about. We are sure many people who understood what it means showed it to five other folks, thereby making this simple piece of design all the more effective!

Having explored a plethora of examples, let us now move on to the second approach.

Combining with Other Techniques: Negative Space and Perception Shift

One of the amusing aspects of typography is that it can be used in combination with some of the other techniques we have discussed so far: negative space and perception shift.

To recall one example where this has already been demonstrated, turn to the last example presented in Chapter 5. By manipulating the word 'Save' in order to depict a water droplet in the negative space, the Save Water idea already achieves this effect. Similarly, many other avenues of design exist, whereby elements can be hidden within the negative spaces created by letters, to exude a second meaning.

A popular example of the same is the logo of FedEx:

Look at the negative space created by the clever placement of the letters 'E' and 'x'. You will notice a forward arrow signal there, which is a metaphor for the value that the logistics company brings to their customers. Clever, isn't it?

Let us now explore a few examples of this approach, but specifically in the realm of perception shift, to see how words can be manipulated along with external elements or by themselves to create visuals that give it an additional meaning.

If you have gotten a decent idea of how the technique of PS can be combined with typography, you would have already noticed that one example of the same has been covered in the chapter. Can you recall it? If not, we suggest that you skim through the previous few pages, it really isn't hard to detect.

But if you are lazy (like us) and prefer us to lay it out straight, here is the answer: the Father's Day design, the one with which we kicked off this chapter. The tweak made to the apostrophe sign to resemble a sperm is a textbook case of perception shift. That said, let us look at a few more interesting ways of doing it.

We would first like to showcase what might be one of our most famous designs of all time. The way to measure it is not only the traction it got on our channels but how much it was replicated and the reach it garnered globally. Let us talk about that in a minute, once we have witnessed the sheer simplicity of the idea.

The event that was the subject of this idea was something that grabbed the entire world's attention. At the end of March 2021, we all witnessed a traffic jam that impacted the entire world.

We are referring to the crisis that occurred when a ship got blocked at the Suez Canal and brought the movement of global cargo to a standstill.

It was a supply chain shock of massive proportions and there was panic all over the place. Even though the issue got resolved a few days later, the conversations on the internet resembled nothing short of a harrowing frenzy. It occurred to us that this was yet another topic of attention for everyone on a global scale and that it presented a nice, little opportunity to spit out an interesting piece.

It may seem like what we are presenting is the only way to do it but that is not so. A variety of ideas were attempted, but what we ended up finalising captivated all of us quite strongly. It was a simple typographical play that manipulated the letters in the word 'Suez' to visually represent the block, thereby creating one of the cleverest perception shift typographies in a very long time. Here's what it looked like:

If Suez Canal had a new logo

Just a teeny bit of adjustment in the 'Z' and we got a perfectly minimal visual to show what was happening up there! The creative was naturally very appealing and it immediately went viral. But the way it spread was something that even we had not anticipated.

Numerous people edited our logo out of the design and started posting it on their handles. Content pages with millions of followers were doing this; it was not only happening in India. It was a global thing! Proof of this contagion was observed on platforms like Reddit, where this was being shared around with captions in different languages which we were not able to comprehend. Whatsapp stories went up, people started reaching out to us personally since they were awestruck by the design, and even celebrities and famous entrepreneurs began sharing this on social media. On our own page, this ended up reaching hundreds of thousands of people, but that was simply the tip of the iceberg.

Enough of the impact figures though. Let's look at what worked here—the factors that clicked and resulted in the immense virality. To begin with, we must acknowledge a factor that goes beyond the design: timing. As a team, we were quick to arrive at and execute this idea. It went live at a time when the issue was smoking hot, and all the hype around it naturally added fuel to the fire. In a sense, we certainly were lucky to have experienced such a wildfire of likes, comments and shares. We are grateful to one of our senior team members who enthusiastically took this task upon himself, even though it was a weekend and he was scheduled to grab a few (dozen) beers with his friends.

Talking purely about the design, we want to highlight a couple of finer details that designers must pay attention to in order to achieve masterful execution. Just a few points that are not so obvious:

1. The word 'Canal' was eliminated and we stuck only to 'Suez' because it was better and more focused. Moreover, the second word was not even needed to do the magic, and in hindsight, it was a prudent call to stick only to what was necessary. That is, after all, the core principle of minimalism. In fact, the initial idea was to show the same blockade in the 'N' of 'Canal', but then the same was seen to be possible in 'Z', thereby eliminating the need for the second word itself. For all you know, this alternative idea might not have been all that popular!

2. Notice the finesse with which the PS has been executed. The shadows are adding a subtle impact to the design. The choice of font also is critical because the rest of the unmanipulated letters have to look congruent with the manipulated letter 'Z'.

3. One of the other really critical elements in the design was a clever wall copy. 'If Suez had a new logo', this was perfect because it gave people a line that they could themselves use while taking screenshots or simply snipping it and posting it on their social channels/chat groups. It also had a quirkiness that further sparked the contagion. It has long been our observation that a copy that makes people laugh works wonders as people start directly using it when they share the creative

These are just some of the things that worked in this idea's favour. As we have been saying, many other tips and tricks for execution shall be covered in the last two chapters of the book.

This entire episode was just unprecedented for us. But the story does not end here. As you would know by now, it never does!

A few days later, the blockage got cleared and the ships were back on track once again. Since the conversation was being so keenly followed everywhere, even this piece of news was doing the rounds. Latching on to the opportunity, as it is a part of our nature now, we came up with another creative to mark the peaceful end of the saga that had kept the world tense and wide awake for a week:

This was again a typographical response to what had happened, but not the kind where we used PS. It had merely utilised the 'Zzz' symbol to showcase that the world would finally sleep peacefully now that the Suez crisis was behind us.

Granted, this design does not come close to the ingenuity and originality of the previous one. Nevertheless, it received

Finally, the (shipping) world can sleep peacefully.
Ever Given has crossed the canal smoothly!

good traction on social media, more so for our quick and clever response and for creating a whole new 'minimalist' conversation on a world event. That was what ended up impressing many, and we had a wonderful week full of business inquiries from some well-known brands. A job well done, we would like to believe!

Let us now witness another smart example of PS used in conjunction with typography. This one was when a black hole was sighted and its pictures were flooding all over the digital world. This happened in April 2019 and coincidentally, it was also the time of general elections in the country. Combining the two disparate events, our team crafted a clever message:

Don't let your country's future go into the black hole

This was again a clever usage of a trending event to deliver an important public message. Here again, you'd see how the wall copy does a great job of complementing and even enhancing the idea, tying together the two unconnected events in a thoughtful manner.

From a technical perspective, the designer can note how the 'O' in the word 'Vote' was perceived as an opportunity to incorporate the black hole visual. A doubt may now arise in your mind. We had rejected a very similar approach while evaluating ideas for the Elon Musk design. As you would recall, incorporating the Mars visual into the 'O' of Elon (explored in the section on expressive typography) was dismissed.

So how did we end up doing the exact same thing here? In fact, the same idea looks quite nice in this context. What is the difference? A couple of them, in fact, that makes the 'Vote' typography much better than the other idea:

- The biggest difference, to begin with, is how the Vote idea cleverly uses the black hole image, including the background, as the core focal point. It is more like the typography is being superimposed on the image of a black hole rather than the other way around (which happens to be the case for the rejected Elon idea). Inverting the approach actually made the Vote idea much fresher than it would have been, had we tried to box a visual and constrain it within the typography of the word 'Vote'.

- Building on the previous point, it is easy to identify a black hole given the vivid image at our disposal.

The same is not true for the Mars visual that we were attempting to use.

- A finer point here is that the black hole image is evocative. The O flying-in-the-air-like-Mars image was evocative. There is no such emotion elicited by a simple Mars being shown in the word 'Elon'. To put it more crudely, it did not really feel like anything very different from the forms of creativity most typically observed on the internet.

- One final and crucial point here, as we have already mentioned in passing, is that the beauty of the vote idea springs from the fact that it connects two disparate and totally unrelated issues with a strong design-copy combination. The rejected Elon idea, on the other hand, makes the most obvious connection and delivers it in a rather direct manner. There is no veiled or hidden message which, in some ways, is one of the crucial hallmarks of our signature approach to minimalism. It also seems like the first idea that would occur to anyone trying to create something engaging on the topic, which is what qualifies it for auto-rejection!

Having reflected deeply on these points we shall now move our attention to Ambigrams, one of the most unique weapons in our arsenal, and one of the most criminally under-utilised tools in the world of (typographical) design.

Ambigrams

Ambigrams are arrangements of word(s) that can be interpreted in multiple ways. Once again, we are greeted by the shadow of perception shift! The key difference here, though, is that the multiple interpretations are all typographical—that this is a technique that exudes meanings purely based on words and not any visuals (as we explored in the previous section).

Ambigrams come in many varieties. For instance, if you flip a word and can see the exact same word, it is termed as a *rotational ambigram*. If you can see the same word even if you look at its mirror image, it is called a *mirror ambigram*. Ambigrams can also be multilingual: where you can read multiple interpretations but in different languages. A good example of this was the Agra-Taj design showcased in Chapter 2. You can read 'Agra' in Devanagri and 'Taj' in English, thereby incorporating two different scripts within the design. Chirag happens to be an expert in this field and has even published a few papers. The technical jargon for the Agra-Taj design, which he presented in a nerdy design talk at IDC, IIT Bombay, seven years ago, is 'multilingual perceptual shift ambigram'. Quite a mouthful, we know.

This section is aimed at exploring some varieties of ambigrams and how they can be used towards the end goal of creating inventive, minimal content. In doing so, we shall explore a wide range of examples that have gone live on The

Minimalist's social handles and attracted not only positive attention but a ton of curiosity as well.

Let's start with one of our earliest examples. This was back in 2015 in the heydays of the Indian startup ecosystem. Investor money had been flooding into new-age tech startups, which was resulting in rapid expansion and nosebleed valuations for young upstarts. However, winter was not far away and the bubble soon popped, at least in the short term. What followed was a short period of austerity marked by downsizing, several startups going kaput and most visibly, a round of brutal layoffs across the board.

We watched with amazement as big companies shrivelled in size and distressing downsizing pieces made the news every day. It was also quite paradoxical that companies that were rolling in the dough just a few quarters ago had taken to drastic cost-cutting measures. Talent that had easily gotten massively high-paying jobs was suddenly asked to leave in a drastic reversal of fortunes. Remarking on the situation, we said that at that stage in time, startup life was rather precarious. 'You could be hired any time, and fired any time.'

Listening to that remark, we both noticed the rhyme. But more than the rhyme, it is the typographical similarity of the two words that caught Chirag's attention. Scribbling in his untidy notebook, he attempted an ambigram with the exact same sentence, to see if a dual meaning could emerge very naturally. Please refer to the facing page to understand what the experiment culminated in.

As you can see, the visual clearly leads to two interpretations: 'At startups you can be hired any time' and 'At startups you can be fired any time'. Using an ambigram to create the dual perception is where the trick of minimalism lay in this example. Naturally, this one was widely shared in the startup community, given the topicality of the issue.

But there is more to this idea. It was only after it was executed that we realised that it did not just have two meanings, it had three! You could even interpret it as 'At startups you can be tired any time'! And needless to say, even this interpretation was quite relatable. Just ask the folks burning the midnight oil in early-stage companies! Having been there, we can completely attest it.

Therefore, 'dual' is not even the right word for this idea.

It was quite a leap to have used one word to create three meanings: this was probably our first triple perception idea! No wonder it was so hotly shared and became a source of informal banter on numerous groups.

Like most intriguing designs, we framed this one and put it in one of our meeting rooms, given how it always enamoured people and sparked conversations: people loved asking each other their interpretations. However, it was only after a long time that we realised the peculiar placement of this frame. We had placed it quite visibly in the meeting room that was typically reserved for job interviews! Imagine the impact of this placement for a second: people coming to our office for an interview would enter the room and immediately be greeted by a frame that said—you could be hired or fired anytime! What a fabulous first impression, right?

Indeed, even people who live, breathe and eat design make really silly mistakes. That is exactly why all your ideas, even the ones you are confident will win for you an Oscar or a Cannes, should be regularly stress tested with a bunch of fresh eyes. The uninitiated can notice errors that our eyes have gotten accustomed to and just can't identify! We shall discuss this further in the last chapters of the book.

Another example is a design that our team came up with on National Science Day. Now, it is a known fact that most folks who gravitated towards the world of design, marketing and creativity most likely struggled with subjects like science (and mathematics—that haunted subject) in school. The times when this was mostly vividly demonstrated was the viva examinations, when almost all questions of our teachers were met with silence—pure golden silence.

Given that most of our memories of science were tarnished by that deafening silence during vivas, our team made a quirky design out of this correlation: something that millions of science-fearing youngsters would immediately relate to:

From vivas to exams, silence is what science invoked! #NationalScienceDay

Within the same visual, one can read 'Silence' right off the bat. But a slightly more careful look, aided by the wall copy, leads us to observe that one can also read 'Science' at the same time! The genesis of this idea came from two acute observations. It all began with the mind map and, while staring at the word 'Science', it was noticed that the last four letters—ence—could be used to attempt a rhyme. That is when we realised that 'Silence' is a word that ends exactly with those same letters (even though it does not really rhyme).

Additionally, it has the exact same number of total letters, making it ripe for an ambigram attempt! Thus began the exploration, which led to the final output.

Based on our extensive research and work with ambigrams and typography, we ended up creating an entire new class of ambigrams, an IP that utilised different techniques to take perception shift to a whole new level. We christened the idea of a 'dynagram'. Let us explain what that means briefly.

A dynagram is an arrangement of words which, just like an ambigram, gives rise to a different meaning when manipulated. What we ended up incorporating into the usual definition of ambigram is the power of animation. We thereby created a motion graphic property in the world of ambigrams that would utilise both rotation and revolution in its elements to achieve its new state. Since a book might not be the best medium to understand what a dynagram is like, we shall leave QR Codes with our examples so that you can experience those creations online. We will, of course, show images of the starting and ending slate of the dynagrams, but the real magic of perception can only be witnessed by looking at the animation.

One of our most popular dynagrams was one that we created for India's most beloved cricket captain: MS Dhoni. On the day of his retirement, we wanted to create a piece that showed just how much he meant to India.

In the course of our ideation sessions, we realised that some of the letters of the word 'Dhoni' could easily be manipulated (via rotation and revolution) to make them look like India.

We would strongly recommend that you first check out this dynagram online in all its glory if you have a device close by. Here's the link for your viewing pleasure.

Here are the static snapshots that showcase the mechanics of this dynagram:

And finally, transforms to:

Static visuals just cannot do justice to the delight produced, so we would strongly recommend you check out the actual animation on the QR Code provided on the previous page.

With this, we have arrived at the end of our thoroughly enjoyable typography journey. Now, having seen so many examples and approaches, it's time for you to put your brain to work and unleash your creativity to build a unique typographical idea of your own.

Practice Net

Challenge #3: Come up with a typography-based design idea for Valentine's Day.

CHAPTER 7

Humour

Let us now begin our journey of what might be the most interesting chapter of them all. In this chapter, we shall work our way through numerous ways to utilise humour in order to create compelling content and communication. This might also be the most accessible chapter to readers—there are no design technicalities that we need to understand to make the most of this.

We began the last chapter by asking an important question: 'Who said that good design necessarily requires visuals?' It was an important question to ask. We then went through an entire chapter dedicated to the craft of typography—something that Chirag had been honing ever since he entered college. Since he was not a graphic designer by training, typography was naturally a much easier and more approachable route for him to create thought-provoking work. No need to come up with detailed illustrations or highly intricate visuals—he simply figured out a way to stick to the bare minimum—manipulation of letters and words to create stuff that was inventive.

This chapter will take that approach even further and introduce you to the toolkit of humour: because when you can't design *at all*, you can resort to techniques of humour which can later be packaged into a nice minimal design. This is what Sahil did since the earliest days of The Minimalist. With absolutely no background in design, Sahil was adept only at posting lame jokes on Facebook. Importing the same skill set into this endeavour, he realised that a lot of value could be created by producing an explosive combination of design and humour.

Here are some approaches that the chapter is broken down into. These approaches are quite substrate-independent. They can be used for minimalist design or to write one-liners or even in poems and long-form writing. The substrate (the medium where these techniques manifest themselves) does not matter, the techniques do. This is why we claimed that this is a general purpose chapter. For the purpose of this book, we shall stick to the domain we started out with (minimalist design) and showcase how they can result in some lovely, viral ideas.

Wordplay

We all understand what it means. Wordplay is just a play of words. The trick here is to do it in a way that adds a totally different meaning to the context with the smallest and most easily fitting play possible. That will become clear with the following example, which was made some years ago:

See the play? The subtle change that was done here was to turn 'typing' into 'stereotyping'. With one tiny modification, we had an explosive idea at hand, which was clear because of the thousands of shares that this got within hours. It'd clearly struck a chord, and it was evident when people started using the phrase 'Family is stereotyping' in comments and while sharing!

Now, this entire idea was born when one of us noticed that 'typing' could have such a drastic change in meaning with the addition of a simple prefix. To make the most clever use of this observation, the modified word was placed at a place where one would *not expect it*: an automated system message.

> *That's the trick—ideas are doubly more delightful if they emerge from unexpected places. We're all used so seeing '<Name> is typing' on our interfaces. That default machine message is what made it so ripe for a clever wordplay.*

Constructing the rest of the context was relatively simple. We simply had to place a short message to the family that most directly represents the situation where such stereotyping takes place. What also makes this idea even more hard-hitting is the meaning that the wordplay elicits: that the family has started stereotyping in their minds already! For some, it was quite an accurate and hilarious depiction of the unfortunate reality, which was why it was shared so widely.

Another example of wordplay can be seen in our communication when one of India's largest states instituted a beef ban, which resulted in much hue and cry all over the interwebs. With a light-hearted approach, here's what we posted:

As expected, this also started going viral moments after it was posted. This was a play on the name of a famous TV show called 'The Big Bang Theory'. The visual also uses the logo of that show in a cheeky manner. While this is an example of wordplay, it is also a clever use of pop culture elements to create viral communication, something we'll examine further in the next chapter.

Wordplay is not just a technique to make people laugh. It can also deliver thoughtful messages in a very compelling way, drawing on connections that were hitherto unobserved. After the news of a massive terrorist attack that rocked the world in 2017, we came up with this:

Terror 404.
Peace not found.

You may have noticed that the style of executing the word play is quite similar to the first example. While brainstorming, one of the writers observed that the word terror (which would naturally be at the top of the mind map with such a brief), with just one letter less, reads 'Error'. And that observation led his neural pathways to deliver another connection: Error 404. After all, that's the most common form of error that human beings encounter on a regular basis. So what does that error say? 'Page not found'. That thought was simply modified to 'Peace not found' with the depiction of a planet that was losing blood-—an allusion to the brutal attack that had just taken place.

Thus, from a clever, multi-layered observation and a really parsimonious wordplay, we came up with a thoughtful post on a dark day.

A few recommendations for good wordplay:

- Make the play as natural as possible: like Terror–Error and Typing–Stereotyping. In both cases, the two words rhyme. We have noticed that when that is the case, the play seems very natural and turns out to be quite effective. But beware, in cases where the play is easy to come by, it may have been noticed (and even used) by most people, and you may not have anything unique to work with!

- Be parsimonious. By that, we mean that one must try to make the extent of the play as minimal as possible, so it still retains the original meaning. We have seen wordplays that thoroughly mangle the original word and thereby distance themselves from it. The point of a wordplay is defeated in such cases and it turns out to be not very effective.

- Use it sparingly. Wordplays are like expressive typographies: they should only be used when the idea is truly remarkable and is something that cannot easily occur to other creative folks, and definitely not the first idea that anyone would come up with for a particular brief. It is best to note people's reactions with a quick user-test to see if they laugh/smile (if humour is the direction). If they do not react immediately after seeing what you've done, you know it probably needs some work.

Double Meaning

Let us now use the second approach in the humour arsenal—double meaning. Once again, the meaning is rather obvious: using one word to indicate two different meanings. Here's an example:

Notice that this is a play on the word 'Forward' which has two meanings—'Forward thinking' and 'Whatsapp Forwards'. This idea takes a friendly dig at our habit of forwarding all sorts of garbage on Whatsapp and the emergence of the idea that we are all quite knowledgeable and understand the way the world works with those hoary (and often fake) forwards.

Here's another one. In this case, the double meaning is slightly higher-level and not as direct as in the previous example:

Weddings
where 100 people's food and
2 people's lives are wasted

The play here is actually on the word 'Wasted'. The entire insight came from the fact that tons of food is unnecessarily thrown away in all our big, fat weddings. While staring at the word 'Waste', we had a realisation that hey, wait. All jokes on marriages and the tyranny of wives and men losing their cherished bachelorhood came flooding to our minds. And that's when we realised: that food isn't the only thing that's getting wasted in those damned weddings! The designer of course had fun by throwing in the turban next to the dustbin for hilarious effect.

Let us now turn to an approach that comes most intuitively to us and is often employed by spouses in their daily jibes.

Sarcasm

Sarcasm relies on the power of dissonance to create humour. Dissonance occurs when what the user views is quite different from, and often the opposite of, the message that is emerging from a particular design or idea. One of the best examples of a sarcasm was an idea that went viral during the Diwali of 2016.

Rangolis are commonplace during Diwalis and are an absolute pleasure to look at. But as many a creator knows, people love to unwittingly destroy their work by accidentally walking over it. What results is an absolute mess—a rangoli gone haywire because people were not mindful. What a tragedy! This is a faux pas that happens year after year and yet both parties continue the tradition—the makers continue to create strikingly beautiful rangolis and the destroyers continue to walk all over them and destroy those works of art.

Banking on this insight, we came up with an idea that spoke out in defense of those dedicated rangoli creators in a light-hearted manner. Take a look:

When this came out, people went bonkers. Over 5,000 people shared this on Facebook alone—and we were seeing it do the rounds on Whatsapp rather aggressively. That is just the tip of the iceberg though.

The heights of virality were achieved when we saw people *actually making this rangoli* at their houses and posting pictures online. Many other content pages aped this design (after removing our logo, of course) and we saw this design come up on subsequent Diwalis as well! Till these events transpired, even we were blind to the power of sarcasm in creating such levels of virality.

Here's another example. It is one of the earliest ideas from

The Minimalist, posted in late 2014, when we just had a couple of thousand followers and Sahil had one year of college courses to finish before he could think of spending his entire day on such ideas:

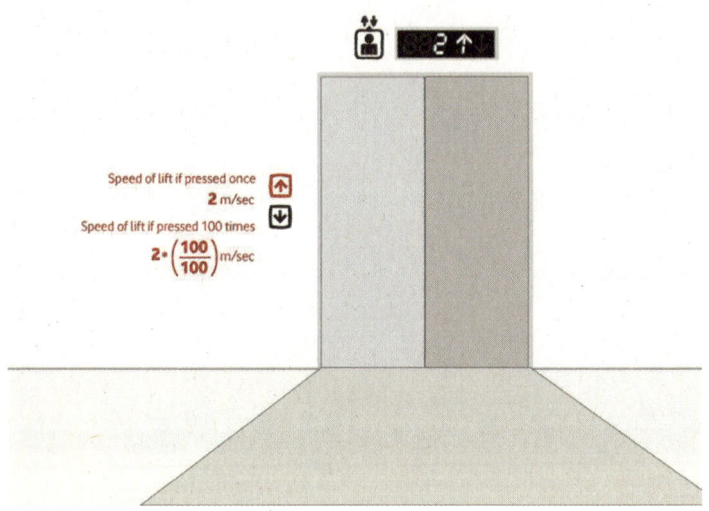

Speed of lift if pressed once
2 m/sec

Speed of lift if pressed 100 times
$2 \cdot \left(\dfrac{100}{100} \right)$ m/sec

The idea is extremely simple. We all know that endlessly pressing the lift button is mindless. Depicting it using a stupid little calculation that subtly points to the stupidity of the habit makes the presentation of that insight quite unique and delightful.

Let us now look at a rather unused approach which can also be put to effective use to induce guffaws.

Exaggeration

Exaggeration is an art. We see it in action in many daily conversations but it feels funny only on some occasions. There's a trick to make it effective. Let us look at a couple of examples where we used exaggeration and multiplied its effectiveness with minimalist design.

The first one is on how many media firms, in the pursuit for eyeballs, end up creating endless sensation and terming anything under the sun as 'Breaking News'. We essentially wanted to create an exaggerated depiction of the media's own exaggerated sensationalism, and here's what it looks like (if you're reading this with kids, it might be a good time to send them for a walk):

Yes, this is for real. And people actually loved this one. The fact that some outlets will pick up absolutely anything for their news pieces was taken to an absurd extreme in this design, which is exactly what makes it rather funny and provocative. The effect of holding out mics and cameras to the most unexpected of displays enhances the humorous effect—it's so out of the ordinary that the dissonance elicits an instant reaction from the audience.

Next up is another example, but this time we'll keep it safe for work. You can get your kid back for this one. When news of record-breaking pollution levels in Delhi came out, our team wanted to come up with something hard hitting. Pictures of the smog and absolute lack of visibility flooded social media and we wondered if that could be a motif that we could utilise.

Our minds then turned to the fact that this haze was rather unnatural and it was an effect imposed on top of the natural reality of the city. Someone immediately drew a connection between how this was like an added layer, almost like a filter on Instagram! Latching on to this insight, the designers did some quick work and ended up posting this on our Instagram page:

Comparing the hazy reality of Delhi to filters was a very novel idea, and our community lapped it up immediately. Tens of thousands of likes poured in within a matter of hours, thanks in part to the sharp timing of this idea. Now some may say that the reality is actually that bad but technical details aside, this is a good example of how the exaggeration approach can be used cleverly.

Let us now turn to the final section of this chapter.

Pop Culture References

This section is all about the effective utilisation of the elements of pop culture that can be smartly incorporated to create clever and well-timed communication. We all live in a hyperconnected world where multiple ideas have taken root in our collective imagination. Hence, there is a massive bank of references that we, as creative people, can latch on to communicate ideas on a particular brief or event.

Technically speaking, using pop culture references is not necessarily a unique approach in the humour toolbox. It is more of a meta-approach and any of the above approaches to humour can be coupled with pop culture references to create explosive content. For that matter, the example that we just saw, the Delhi filter design, also utilised a pop culture element. The Insta story interface is nothing but an element of popular culture: an idea, an interface that most millennials are familiar with and are in the habit of using on a regular basis. So it is safe to say that such an idea is known to most of the audience and can be leveraged for our concepts. That's exactly what we did: leverage the Insta story interface and combine it with the Delhi haze to create something provocative.

Initially, we were going to dedicate a separate chapter on the usage of pop culture elements. But since most examples where we did that effectively involved some form of humour to achieve its end, we thought of placing it in this one itself.

This can, therefore, act as a good summarisation of the ideas discussed so far and is also a meta-technique to keep in mind while creating content.

Here's an example that will still feel a little topical, given the impact it has had on our lives. Just when the world went into lockdown and we all adapted to the reality of working from home, there was a sudden surge in companies organising webinars. Buoyed by the success of this concept, many more started doing the same—until all our calendars were just chock-full of webinars and it seemed that mankind had suddenly become addicted to them. To show this connection in a hilarious way, here's what the team came up with:

The latest addiction in town

As you must have noticed, the actual approach here is wordplay. Some smart cookie noticed that 'Webinar' ends with 'Nar', which could be easily extended with just three more letters to create a connection with Narcos, a popular TV show. In fact, there was an entire series of ideas that linked TV show names to the realities of working from home which can be seen on our social handles.

Let us now turn to an example that we came up with when

tensions were escalating between India and China and resulted, quite naturally, in a display of nationalistic sentiment online. To tap into that conversation, we intended to come up with some light-hearted communication for the kicks (without any malice or strong jingoism):

**If you mess with us,
Ramesh & Suresh will eat the 5 Star.**

This one was extremely contagious and managed to magically resurface every time tensions with our neighbour escalated! (Just kidding, our team only brought it back again because of its topical appeal). Here, the approach used is double meaning. While noticing China's flag we observed that it has five stars. And it didn't take even a second to quickly relate it to the two characters that have come to represent the 5 Star chocolate brand in India—Ramesh and Suresh.

That is how this idea came alive—just a simple mind map and the conjuring up of a couple of unusual connections, as always!

Again, this idea relied heavily on the awareness of this cultural element (Ramesh and Suresh) being present in our audience's minds. Looking at the traction numbers, it looks like our hunch was correct.

Here's an example that was not done in response to any topical event but was rather a part of a series on how superstitions continue to hold sway over our minds. In India, we are all aware of this particularly weird notion that if you cross a black cat's path, bad luck will befall you. It is rather hilarious. We wanted to use this superstitious idea and relate it some social issue to deliver a strong public message, so here's what we did (refer to the image on the next page).

Building on the idea that we just don't obey traffic rules, this idea is a humorous suggestion that only the superstitious fear of crossing a black cat's path can make us stop when the signal is red. Amusing, isn't it? Delivering two messages with one idea.

The cultural element here is the superstition of course. Remember, pop culture does not just mean cool TV shows, web series', movies and sports events. It includes any idea that is known by the masses with sufficient clarity for us to utilise it in our communication. Despite addressing urban audiences and millennials, this and other ideas in the series on superstitions were widely appreciated because people were aware of them. Without that knowledge, these posts would most likely have flopped.

The next idea is again an old one that utilised a pop culture element from the Batman franchise. We wanted to create a social communication on the scourge of tobacco spitting. Take a look at the image on the next page.

We all have seen those disgusting red patches of tobacco decorating our walls. By shaping it in the form of Joker's smile and using his dialogue ('Do you want to know how I got these scars?') in a modified manner, we were able to drive home the message in a clever way. Once again, this idea relied heavily on people's knowledge of Joker— the smile, his famous dialogue and all that. But given the raging sensation that Batman and Joker have been, we didn't even have to think for a second before using those references.

Here's one last example of pop culture being used, albeit for a very different reason. In May 2021, our business was growing fast and the team at The Minimalist was scaling up rapidly. Our HR team was constantly searching for the best talent to join the company, and naturally they were using various ways of digital communication to attract talent.

At exactly the same time, anticipation of the Friends Reunion was reaching a maddening frenzy on the internet. Given the show's popularity and appeal, it was trending for quite some time and dominating most of the online conversations for at least a week. Capitalising on the topicality of the event, our team put out a hiring post:

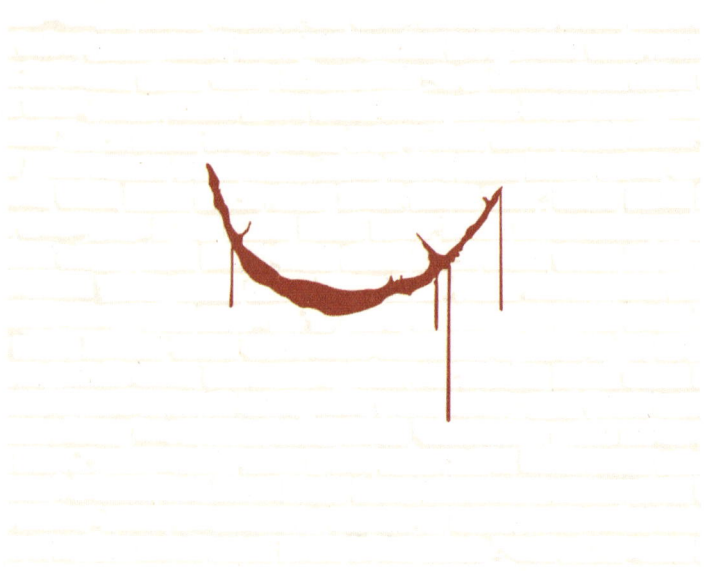

Your spit gave me those scars

The response was mind-boggling. We were just shocked to see the virality that this post achieved. Never have we witnessed a mere hiring post garnering tens of thousands of likes and achieving such a tremendous amount of traction! The impact was naturally seen on our HR ID, as the job application floodgates opened up. Isn't it amusing how creative content can be put to work even in areas one would barely imagine to be relevant?

Having enjoyed so many diverse examples, it is now time to put the knowledge to work!

tell your

F·R·I·E·N·D·S

we are hiring

So they can have a reunion with
all of their coolest ideas and see them
turn into reality!

Practice Net

Challenge #4: Use some pop culture or
relatable elements to come up with a
humorous idea on the shenanigans and
funny things that happen on office calls.

PS- You can use the interfaces of Zoom,
Google Meet and MS Teams to come up
with something.

CHAPTER 8

Interactive Content

This chapter is all about creating content that does not restrict itself to visuals or animations but goes a step further to involve the user—making them do something to get to the final message of the creative. By invoking their curiosity and delivering a satisfying solution in the end, interactive content has even more potential to be shared and achieve virality on platforms like Instagram as well as short-video platforms.

Here's an example of how one can get the users involved. On World Yoga Day, this is what our team posted (refer to the image on the facing page).

On the face of it, this looks like an intense yoga pose of a headstand. But if you rotate and see this thing (as the post asks you to do), you will see the same person lying down and sleeping on the pillow! Banking on the insight that we're all too lazy to do yoga and end up just lazing around on our beds, this concept ensured that the user was asked to participate in the process of uncovering the perception shift by turning their phones!

Rotate your phone to find out your favourite Monday yoga pose
#InternationalYogaDay

Here's another one. In February 2018, things were getting intense between America and North Korea and a lot hinged on a meeting between Trump and Kim Jong Un. Since that time coincided with V-Day, here's what our team posted:

The interactive element here is that when you double tap on Instagram, the heart appears at the centre of the screen- and it lands exactly above the hands of the two men! Here's what people liking this see:

#HappyValentinesDay

This was a clever utilisation of the double tap feature which added a layer on top of the existing design to complete the idea—and it reaches the stage only when the user taps and interacts with the post! This creates a unique social media content experience, unlike anything they've seen!

Next up is one of the most interesting and hilarious examples of creating interaction and getting the audience itself to generate some ridiculously funny content that makes the idea even better. On 1 April 2020, this is what we posted:

No caption, nothing, just April 1, 2020 written with a crpytic shadow. It was up to the users now to figure out what the heck we were trying to say. Now, on the first of April, everyone's aware of attempts to fool them, but this one was a curveball. To be fooled, you first need to know what someone's saying, based on which, you can then try to decipher how they are lying to you or misleading you. But in this case, what we were trying to say itself was vague. What followed was a comments-section discussion of epic proportions.

Many innocent folks openly admitted that they were struggling to make sense of it and asked what this meant. Some creative ones went on to derive some solid interpretations—how it was a shadow because of the sun, how it represented a shadow being cast on the economy and all sorts of hilarious prepositions that reminded us of our Eighth Grade English poem interpretations.

Some even played along and said things like 'Wow, this is pure genius' and 'Damn! Took me a while to get it. You guys are amazing'. This threw others in a tizzy as they struggled to make sense of it. But in the end, we were pretty sure everyone realised that there was absolutely no meaning baked into this one!

It was just an attempt to unleash people's creativity and have fun in the process. We were quite successful in that endeavour as people had a gala time flooding the comments section with their epic responses. Talk about getting your users to themselves make up the content for a post!

Mideos

To end this chapter, we also want to shed light on a new avenue for using the techniques of minimalism: videos. Predicting the rise of short video formats, we had conceptualised an IP called 'Mideos'. Short for minimal videos, this was supposed to be a content format that utilised the same techniques that we have discussed but in video format to bring out hard-hitting messages in 10-15 seconds. We came up with this term before Facebook launched its thumbstoppers idea, and ended up shooting some innovative content on issues like smoking, domestic violence and respect for the army. Take a look at some of QR codes on the next page so that you can check out this format.

These are just some of the ways in which the audience can be involved in the content. We encourage you to explore different social media elements and features so that they can be incorporated within the creative concepts that you come up with. It's now time for our next task.

Practice Net

Challenge #5: *Assume that you have been transported back to the early days of COVID-19 and are experiencing a nationwide lockdown. Create some interactive content using some new elements that engages your audience.*

CHAPTER 9

Mastering Execution

It has been quite a journey looking at the multifarious techniques and approaches that one can employ in their journey of minimalism. In this chapter, we shall now turn our attention to two things—how you can improve your own perception so that such ideas come to you more naturally and how you can master the execution phase once the ideas are in place.

Techniques to Improve Perception

When people see the content created by The Minimalist and even learn the techniques that have helped us, there is still that nagging feeling: 'Even though I see how you did it, how can *I start seeing things the way you guys do*, so I can start making such content myself?' It is a completely valid question. Even an understanding of the techniques that went into our ideas might not be enough to start churning out great ideas every day. That is why we have some suggestions: not on the techniques this time, but on perception. Just like beauty, all creative interpretation also lies in the eyes of the beholder. We shall now share some techniques that can help you see things better and interpret them differently. Once you practice them and start getting better, applying the techniques mentioned in this book will become more like muscle memory: an automatic, unconscious process where your brain starts forming connections that were hitherto unnoticed.

1. Stare: Staring at objects for long periods of time has most certainly allowed us to see them differently. This is the first step in altering your perception. Stare at real-life objects. Stare at the visuals on the mind map you have. Stare at different kinds of representations of the object by doing a Google image search and seeking out different forms. It is only when we look at objects for extended periods of time that we start noticing things that we didn't notice initially, and start forming patterns that the untrained and impatient eye can never expect to. Staring at a tea cup for a long period (even though some may perceive that as a sign of madness) resulted in the observation of the cricket stumps hidden in its anatomy (as shown in Chapter 4). Staring at the Indian map is also what led to the observation that the seven North-Eastern states are high-fiving the rest of the country. This resulted in a beautiful concept that gained immense popularity in our early days.

2. Squint: It is a well-known secret of perception that

**The
high five
of UNITY**

everything we see is not really what we are seeing but
what our brains are telling us. So if you are staring at
a bottle on the table, your brain is guessing that the
input entering its system most likely represents a bottle,
which is why it can be difficult to see it as something
else beyond just a bottle: that's literally what your brain
wants you to see it as. So the trick to seeing differently
is to mess up your brain's guessing system. Squinting
(or seeing things with one eye closed) can alter what
you are seeing and thereby lead to perceiving the same
object differently.

3. Rotate/Invert: Many times, we just need to change the orientation of objects we are staring at to see things differently. We often see the power of this idea when some cards or pages are kept upside down, and we can suddenly read something completely different from what's written there. Ambigrams are very easy to build this way. The same action, when performed on objects, can be a great incubator for perception shift-based ideas.

4. Reduce: Most often, our eyes get lost in the details of what we are seeing, which hinders our ability to directly observe the basic shapes and forms that make them up. Staring at a picture of a whale you may get lost in its vivid colours and features—details which will move you away from detecting fundamental forms which can be tweaked to give rise to an alternate perception. Staring at a bare-bones vector form of a whale instead, we managed to see that the tiny little space representing its mouth was cylinder-shaped, and could be manipulated to hide a water bottle there. Reduction also helped us to see that a sickle is essentially a curved shape, very similar to the R in Hindi. By adding a few lines, we could make it look like a rupee sign: and that's exactly what we did in the idea that went viral during the Farmers' Protest (Chapter 4).

5. Deconstruct: Every object in your mind map, be it a visual if you are attempting perception shift or a word

if you are attempting expressive typography, should be deconstructed. What we mean is that one must learn to observe the individual elements that make up the whole. As we saw, perception shift can happen inside the object or outside—when it happens inside (as in the World Animal Day example in Chapter 4), one must start separating out the elements that make up an object and stare at them individually. Isolating the shapes of the continents from the globe is what allowed us to notice that the map of South America could somehow be construed as a flying bird. Similarly, looking at the word 'Save', we deconstructed it by noticing all the empty gaps in the typography, that is, all the negative spaces that could be exploited for creating an alter-perception. The curved space within 'a' seemed ripe for modification and ended up becoming a drop of water (Chapter 5).

Practice these on a regular basis every time you get to work and you will gradually find yourself improving your observational skills. Perceptions will come alive in a way as never before and your brain will foster new connections with increasing speed as the practice deepens. Having repeated this process for over half a decade now, we can attest to the fact that one's skill can dramatically improve over time with long periods of ideation, iteration and getting feedback from other designers. We have also used the same approach in numerous training sessions and have seen many members in our company emerge as champions in the craft of minimalism.

However, many of those designers and content writers never underwent a lot of formal training and instruction; they learned merely by participating in regular brainstorming sessions and starting to see things the way we liked to see them. If they could learn via mere observation, we are confident that you certainly would, given the entire retinue of techniques and practices that you've now been handed. Let us now turn to the second important aspect: mastering execution.

Mastering Execution

This section is geared more towards the finer details of execution: how one can pay attention to the details and bring in a measure of finesse and class to the design once an idea has been formulated. Given the nature of the discussion, this will be most relevant for designers, art and creative directors, and anyone whose job needs them to provide creative input and be responsible for the quality of design in any communication projects. If you're not going to be involved in the design execution phase, you may skip this section.

If you look at the way minimalist designs usually look, you would feel they are really easy to execute because, well, they don't contain a lot of stuff. Actually, that's far from the truth.

When you have a limited visual canvas, you have to ensure everything is pixel perfect. However, one can easily master the art of making pixel perfect designs with regular practice and by following some of these recommendations:

1. Colours: When it comes to execution, your colour scheme is the most critical thing on your canvas. A significant fraction of people decide whether to check your design or not based on the kind of colours you have used. When we started The Minimalist, we had a very strong reason for using the colour red for our brand. The idea was to provoke action, so we thought of choosing a colour that would have a thumb-stopping effect. In hindsight, we feel that by consistently sticking to that colour, we have managed to build a very unique brand language that people can recognise even if our logo has been removed. Having said that, we still experiment with a lot of colours because in many cases, one specific colour does not do justice to the communication. A cursory glance at our content will reveal that we have explored various colours based on the specific context in which a creative was made. Let us look at this example to demonstrate how colour choices can be made effectively. The following design highlights how girls are subjected to a lot of terms and conditions. To drive this point home, we came up with a hard-hitting caption: "Being a girl child is

The post that went live

The asterisk in this design would be hard to interpret as a ribbon due to the colour combination used. Our original red colour is taking the focus away from the main object.

subject to illogical risks, please read the patriarchal documents carefully."

2. Fonts: Choosing the correct font in your communication is the second most important piece, especially in designs where you are communicating your message using expressive typography, wordplay, ambigrams, etc. Just like humans have been categorised into 16 different personality types, every font also has its own personality. You have to pick the right font as per the target audience, tone and objective of your communication. You would be surprised to know that font psychology is actually a big research topic.

At its heart, font psychology is all about understanding different emotions associated with various fonts and using them to your advantage. For example, when we use Gotham in our communication it gives a very modern, professional and stable feel to the design which would be very different from, say, using Garamond or Baskerville or Comic Sans. If all of this is Greek or Latin to you, don't worry. By learning some font basics and doing a bit of practice and experimentation, these things will become clearer over time.

A lot of times, you might have to build some custom letters to perfectly match the mood of your design. Perfectly executed ambigrams and dynagrams usually require custom typography and you will have to master the pen tool in Illustrator to execute some of them with utmost finesse.

Given the focus on fonts in minimalist communication, one has to find a perfect balance in terms of kerning, leading and tracking in the design. These are all nothing but ways to manipulate the spacing between characters. These special adjustments are an important tool to help create better readability and a more aesthetically pleasing design. A lot of times a perfectly kerned word can represent your idea in a much better way than a normally written word with default kerning. It is very important to experiment with these little things to find the perfect balance in your typography.

If you are new to the field of typography, here are some detailed definitions of these intimidating jargons:

Kerning: It is the adjustment of the space between two individual letters horizontally, to help the text become more readable and aesthetically pleasing.

Tracking: Tracking, which also involves horizontal spacing, is the adjustment of spacing throughout the entire word.

Leading: It is the design element of typography that determines how text will be spaced vertically in lines when your text is to be written in multiple lines.

One other important aspect of typography which

KERNING

LEADING
LEADING
LEADING

TRACKING

has to be kept in mind is the size of the font which you are using. In many situations, you have to design communication that will be viewed on mobile, laptop, desktop or print together. Choosing the right font size, which will make the text visible, is quite important.

Here is an example where we have picked the right font based on our experimentation:

If you look at both of these fonts closely, you will see that the typeface in the first design makes it more contextual and relatable compared to the second

The design that went live with a font which is more
contextual and clearly perceived as '000's (zeroes)

Font frequently used by us for our designs. The rounded 'ooo's
were a little far from the way people usually perceive 0 (zero)

design. We had also adjusted the spacing between the characters to make the design more numeric. Experiments like these help in deciding the correct type for your design.

3. Animation Transitions: Motion graphics in minimalism is one of the most exciting parts for people interested in animation. To make these transitions perfect, you need to simply follow some basic laws of physics—how collision works, the law of gravity, etc. Try to keep your transitions as natural as possible and they will appeal to your audience. Good design is transparent, and the same applies to good transitions in animation. Rather than distracting the audience, the objective should be to see how one can add more value to the idea in a very seamless way.

4. Refining Edges: A lot of times, designers won't notice this but every corner and edge in your design of your visual/text decides the mood of the design. If the corners of the visual are sharp, it will give a different feel as opposed to a design where they are rounded. Even the smallest of the shadows and borders around your visual and text has a big impact. You need to find a balance to see how you can use all of these available degrees of freedom in a way that will keep the visual less cluttered and match the vibe you want to communicate. For example, in the Suez Canal creative, that subtle shadow which

has been added in the slanted line of Z adds a lot of beauty to the visual. It mimics the real situation in a subtle way. As a designer you need to work on such minute details to iterate and elevate your visual by continuously following the Include, Exclude and Focus methodology.

5. Alignment, Placement and Aspect Ratio: Alignment of text and placement of visual elements is always important in any kind of communication but when it comes to minimalist communication, it becomes even more important because there are very few elements that are there on the canvas and all of them have to be in sync: like an orchestra to communicate the core message. First, you need to decide whether your copy is the hero of your communication or the visual. The hierarchy of your layout will depend on this decision. Keep in mind the basic principles of eye movement as well as the readability laws of typography and alignment to decide whether the communication should be left, right or centre-aligned. Also, keep a good aesthetic balance between the aspect ratio of your visual and your text size.

6. Logo placement: A logo if not placed correctly in the communication can spoil the entire layout. After careful experimentation, find a good place for your logo which can be used in a consistent way and give a good amount of importance to it. We have been using our logo at

the bottom of our creatives with centre alignment because it does not interfere with the communication while helping us build a consistent brand language. You can also be bold and omit your logo from some of your creatives once in a while when you have built a good brand language. When people start recognising your creatives without your logo, the marketing team has achieved the gold standard of effective brand language usage!

CHAPTER 10

Client Case Studies

In this chapter, we shall showcase some real-life case studies on how the ideas and techniques of minimalism were utilised by some of the biggest brands in the country to create delightful experiences across their marketing, product and design journeys. We shall present a few examples in three main areas: brand design, moment marketing on social media and Interaction Design (UX for web and mobile-based platforms).

Nykaa: Nykaa is a leading beauty and fashion ecommerce company in India. The Minimalist has partnered with Nykaa to drive some of their important marketing initiatives across various digital media platforms. Our moment marketing command centre team took the trending brand communication a notch above by using the tools available in this book, using techniques like double meaning, perception shift, etc. to build some delightful and often viral content. Take a look at some examples:

Use of double meaning of the word mask

Tata AIG: *TATA AIG General Insurance Company Limited is a joint venture company between Tata Group and the American International Group (AIG). It has strongly emerged as one of the most preferred private general insurance companies in India, with several innovative firsts to its credit.*

With a big section of insurance bookings moving to digital platforms, TATA AIG wanted to build a platform that is very simple to use and has a high brand recall value. In India, insurance has been a very overwhelming space for first-time users and for its existing customer base. To simplify the entire process, we went to the roots of minimalism and applied our principle of Include, Exclude and Focus to build the information architecture to make the entire buying journey very simple and clutter-breaking. We simplified the entire information architecture in such a way that the customer can generate a quote in just two clicks.

We also reduced the total time it takes to book insurance with Tata AIG to three minutes by reducing the number of fields in the forms and by using some third-party integrations like Vahan APIs to fetch some of the details in a very simple way.

Insurance policies are complex products that set off specific rules based on user information. So we created an IA to:

1. Help users navigate through the website

2. Find relevant information at the right time

3. Facilitate decision-making

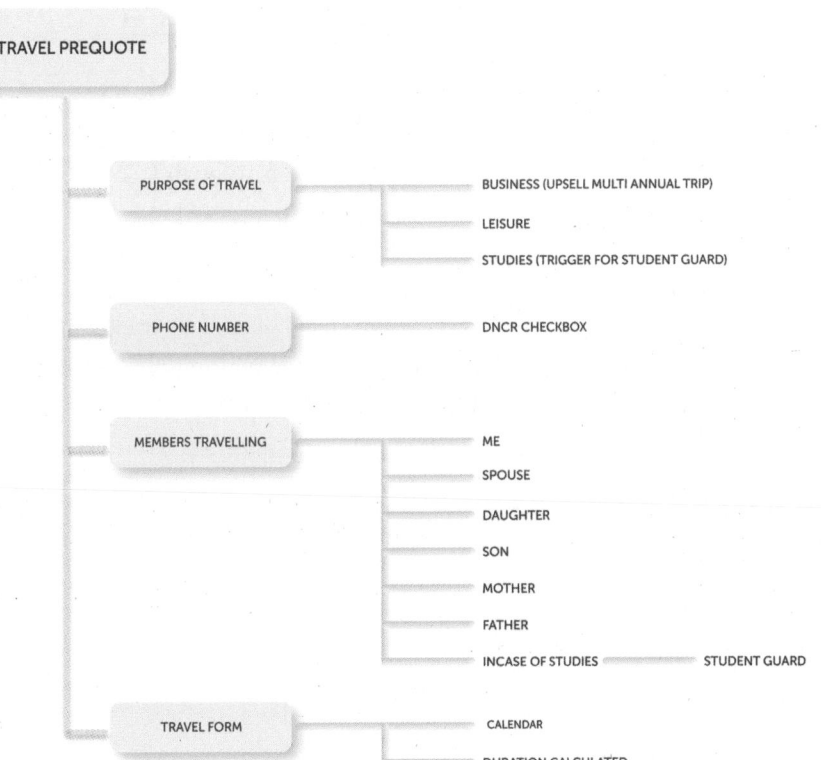

After building a very minimalist and optimized journey for the platform architecture and converting it into wireframes, we initiated the process of building a visual theme that would help in the final representation of the User Interface. While researching, we were quite intrigued by the use of Skeuomorphism in UI design.

Skeuomorphism is a term most often used in graphical UI design to describe interface objects that mimic their real-world counterparts in how they appear and/or how the user can interact with them.

Apple has been using Skeuomorphism in its UI design for a long time now. We thought of implementing a modern version of Skeuomorphism which is popularly known as Neumorphism. We opted for this style mainly to:

- Create a unique and memorable visual language for the digital experience.

- Give a clean and minimal look to the website in an industry which mainly has been focussing on a lot of text and images on their website.

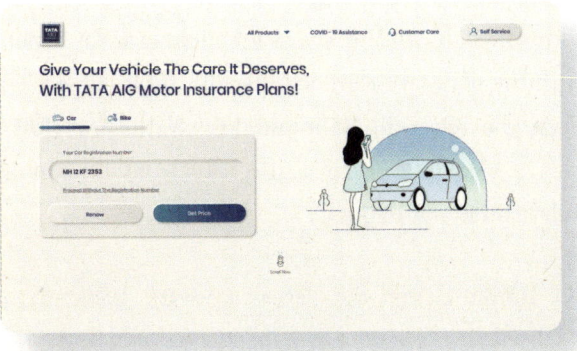

Post the launch, the new digital experience has been driving tremendous results and serves as a benchmark for experience design in the general insurance space in India. Our work has also been the recipient of numerous awards for Best User Experience Design as well as Best Website Design in the General Insurance category.

HDFC Bank: Being the largest private bank in India, HDFC Bank has always been the leader in terms of digital disruption at scale. With so much clutter around in terms of communication around banking, we collaborated with HDFC Bank's marketing team to build a clutter breaking minimalist visual and communication language. We applied some of the principles which we have described in some of our previous chapters: perception shift, expressive typography, dynagrams, etc. to give the brand a very unique tonality on digital platforms.

We took various value propositions of the bank and integrated them with trending moments, festivals and topical days to translate it into thumb-stopping communications. Here are some examples:

An example of a visual dynagram where the visual elements of the logo have been rotated and revolved to form a representation of Lord Ganesha

Let's welcome the God of
new beginnings with HDFC Bank.

#HappyGaneshChaturthi

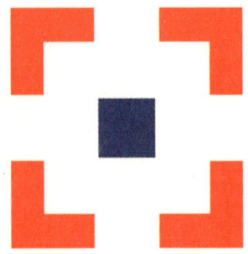

Maintaining social distance yet
being near you 24/7

Effective use of negative space to bring focus on social distancing

Moengage: Moengage is one of India's leading customer engagement and retention platform. Considering the global ambitions of the brand, we were onboarded to craft the brand positioning of the company and translate it into a visual identity. With the space being cluttered, we went back to our roots and applied the same minimalist thinking principles to build a venn diagram around 'What the customers need', 'What the brand has to offer' and 'What competition is offering'. At the intersection of these three spaces, one can find the unique space which the brand can own. For Moengage that space was 'For the customer obsessed marketer'. The essence of the brand was then taken by the design team to develop a compelling and meaningful brand identity. With the clever use of perception shift and negative space, here is the identity that our team built for the brand:

moengage

If you look at the identity closely, you will notice a user in the "o" of moengage. That user in the logo is the representation of the customer and comes directly from their central positioning around customer obsession. We are sure you won't be able to unsee it now once you have observed it.

We specifically decided to include this example to show how the techniques of minimalism can be effectively put to use even in B2B contexts. We've often heard marketers remark that these things are great for customer-facing brands and hard to implement in B2B setups. Our experience suggests that any brand, regardless of the category, can utilise the techniques described in this book to gain an edge over their competitors.

Moengage's redesigned logo on display (Nasdaq in New York)

CHAPTER 11

Back to the Nets

What a journey it has been! We have so far covered various techniques, looked at ideas that will help you improve your perception and master design execution, and even explored the ideas of minimalism in action for real-life client case studies. Having covered everything there is to cover, we will now reveal our responses/ideas to all the challenges mentioned at the end of the chapters that presented each technique.

Please note: there's no single correct way to approach the challenge. Ours is just one out of the hundreds of ways one could tackle the problem statement. You may have developed a completely different idea from the one we are about to present, and if that is indeed the case, we would love to hear from you. After all, we all learn when we see how different people's perceptions lead them to a completely different way of thinking.

Let's dive into all the challenges presented and our solutions now.

Challenge #1: The government has just announced that plastic has been banned and

anyone who's caught using plastic bags can be arrested. Come up with a compelling perception shift on the above topic.

Our response to this is a nice little perception shift between a plastic bag and a person with raised arms—in a manner that's typically seen when people are placed under arrest by the police. The same object is achieving multiple interpretations in this example.

Challenge #2: Use the negative space approach to communicate a powerful message on wildlife conservation.

This example utilises the negative space that you can see between the horns of a deer to symbolise a trophy, proposing that saving them is actually the biggest trophy (this is also a subtle double meaning play in the copy, given how animals are hunted and kept as trophies).

Saving them is the real trophy #NationalWildlifeDay

Challenge #3: Come up with a typography-based design idea for Valentine's Day.

Here's a simple yet devilishly cheeky expressive typography that shows 14 February but picturises its impact (that is felt nine months later) into the visual. We do have some evil minds in the team, no denying that!

Challenge #4: Use some pop culture or relatable elements to come up with a humorous idea on the shenanigans and funny things that happen on office calls.

This idea relies on the interface of meeting apps, which is a key element of popular culture as everybody uses them on a daily basis. This idea depicts the hilarious reality of calls where folks who have their cameras and mics turned off, often have their minds turned off too.

Zoomed in, zoned out

Challenge #5: Assume that you have been transported back to the early days of COVID-19 and are experiencing a nationwide lockdown. Create some interactive content using some new elements that engages your audience.

Our team came up with a beautiful interactive series three months after the lockdown to reminisce the things that we all were missing from our old, 'normal' lives. To do so, the entire series of creatives was linked together by a common element that cut across each of them, creating a sense of continuity and storytelling via design. Here's what the entire frame looks like, but we recommend viewing it on the shared QR code for a better experience:

We hope you enjoyed taking a stab at the problem statements mentioned throughout the book. If you have different ideas on how to approach them, do send us a DM on our Instagram account: @theminimalist_india. Some of the best ideas will even be shortlisted and posted on our page with due credits.

Afterword: Join The Minimalism Movement

When we look back at what has transpired since that fateful day in August 2014, we are filled with immense joy. When we were thinking up stupid names for our page and deciding what we would post, we hardly knew that such a fulfilling journey awaited us. Little did we know that our approach of using minimalism, developing techniques that could repeatedly be used to produce creative delight would snowball not just into a cult following of lakhs of creative enthusiasts but also turn into a national movement.

Sitting in our dirty hostel rooms, we had also started doing something that we did not know would become such a massive trend in just a few years. With all the time in the world to come up with ideas that could make people think, both of us were constantly tracking trending affairs and news pieces we could talk about. That is where ideas like Beef Ban

Theory (Chapter 7) and the Hired-Fired ambigram (Chapter 6) came from and posted right after those events became national news and started trending on social platforms. Essentially, we were doing *moment marketing* before that term even permeated into the consciousness of the Indian marketing, advertising and creative industries. Being at the forefront of this change allowed us to incorporate the same approach for a plethora of brands that wanted to work with us for our unique philosophy, and that is one of the biggest reasons we have managed to grow our organisation into a team of over 170 creative minds. We are immensely grateful for having stumbled upon a method of marketing accidentally, which became a standard part of the marketing plans of all brands.

While we were pushing the boundaries of marketing in our early days, the trend of using minimalism continued to catch on like wildfire. Numerous pages, content creators and brands started emulating our signature style as the trend achieved immense popularity and widespread recognition. It only makes us proud that a stupid little attempt that we decided to stick to, turned into such a massive trend and spawned many followers who started doing the exact same thing, and acting as carriers of our founding philosophy to ever wider audiences. It can clearly be witnessed today in the way brands respond to any viral piece of news that breaks out. If you take one look at the content floating around on the interwebs on such occasions, you will immediately identify brands and content creators using the very same tools of minimalism that we have defined to grab people's attention. That our particular style would become so widespread and omnipresent is something we totally hadn't expected. In fact, there are numerous occasions when people ask us if we created a piece of branded content that has been going viral even when we have not!

At the same time, we are happy that the standard of creativity in India has risen up by a few notches in the preceding years, thanks to the adoption of these approaches at large. It is our hope that we shall continue to innovate via newer and more novel forms of communication and make good design and communication a norm in the country. This book has been our attempt to contribute to this transformation. Even if a handful of designers and creative minds manage to grasp the central ideas presented here, we are confident that they can go on to create really strong communication under diverse circumstances—be it across different mediums, for different audiences and for various brands/initiatives. We can already see a lot of The Minimalist Alumni doing that in various capacities—as entrepreneurs, independent creators, marketing leaders and artists.

Another crucial point to note is that the techniques outlined in this book are not supposed to be utilised only in the way we have shown them. We have decided to showcase the application of the techniques predominantly in the form of social media content, with most ideas utlising vectors or illustrations. However, that is merely the tip of the iceberg. These techniques are medium-independent and can be utlised across various other modes of communication—animation, films, print ads, voice ads, VR ads and what not! We decided to stick to the static visual format simply because that was the norm prevailing in the second half of the previous decade, which is why some of our really popular work happens to be in that format. We have also extended the same principles to formats like GIFs, short videos (Mideos- minimal videos that convey hard hitting messages in much the same way as our statics) and numerous other formats. You will also see the very same techniques at work if you review some of the best print ads or TV commercials, which is what makes these tools and techniques so effective and timeless.

Mediums may come and go, content formats may rise and perish, but the techniques to create inventive ideas will always stay relevant. Having witnessed their power in provoking thought and inspiring action, we hereby urge you to join the minimalist movement so that we can all put more thought into our communication and raise the standards of creativity in the country as well as the world!

About
The Minimalist

Over the past decade, The Minimalist has been at the forefront of creative problem-solving and helping businesses win through inventive solutions.The company was ranked at #8 position in the prestigious LinkedIn Top 25 startups in India. The organisation has grown exponentially since its inception with its offices now in Mumbai, Delhi and London and a team of around 200 creative minds who get up everyday with a single-minded focus of doing inventive work.Some of The Minimalist's notable clients include Coca-Cola, Cadbury, Google, Amazon, Parle, and Swiggy across the domains of:

- Brand Storytelling & Content

- Digital Product & Experience Design (UX/UI)

- Brand Design & Strategy

- Creative Technology(Gen AI, AR, VR, and MR)

- Influencer Marketing & Brand Collaborations

- Video Production: Want to collaborate? Write to hello@theminimalist.in